Legal Manual for Residential Construction

August W. Domel, Jr., Ph.D., J.D.

McGraw-Hill

New York   San Francisco   Washington, D.C.   Auckland   Bogotá
Caracas   Lisbon   London   Madrid   Mexico City   Milan
Montreal   New Delhi   San Juan   Singapore
Sydney   Tokyo   Toronto

pbk   1 2 3 4 5 6 7 8 9 FGR/FGR 9 0 0 9 8 7 6 5

Library of Congress Cataloging-in-Publication Data
Domel, August W. (August William), 1960–
    Legal manual for residential construction / by August W. Domel,
Jr.)
        p. cm.
    Includes index.
    ISBN 0-07-017979-4
    1. Construction industry—Law and legislation—United States.
    2. Construction contracts—United States. 3. House construction-
    -United States. I. Title.
    KF1950.D65 1995
    343.73'078624—dc20
    [347.30378624]   95-18968
                                                          CIP

Acquisitions editor: April D. Nolan
Editorial team: Joanne Slike, Executive Editor
                David M. McCandless, Book Editor
Production team: Katherine G. Brown, Director
                Rhonda E. Baker, Coding
                Rose McFarland, Desktop Operator
                Linda L. King, Proofreading
                Joann Woy, Indexer
Design team: Jaclyn J. Boone, Designer   AN1*
                Katherine Lukaszewicz, Associate Designer   0179794

To my beautiful wife, Gina. She is truly a gift from heaven.

Contents

Introduction

This book provides the contractor with an introduction to the legal forum and is specifically designed to present both the reoccurring legal issues faced by residential and light commercial contractors and the information needed to avoid them.

In order to survive in business, and due to people's propensity in this country to sue each other, the contractor must have some knowledge of the law, especially in the following areas:

➤ Contracts

➤ The litigation process

➤ An alternative to the litigation process

➤ Lien rights

➤ Safety obligations

➤ Zoning and property issues

➤ Choosing a construction attorney

The fourteen chapters and three appendices in this book assist the contractor in understanding these important legal issues and more.

Provided here are brief summaries of each of these chapters and appendices, to orient the reader on the topics to be discussed.

 # Chapter 1—Corporations, partnerships, & sole proprietorships

One of the first decisions confronting an aspiring homebuilder is the format in which to operate the company. Operating a company as a corporation reduces personal liability for losses caused by the business, but it also increases paperwork and possibly the amount of profits lost to taxes. The sole proprietorship is on the other end of the spectrum with respect to these items in that it may allow for less taxes due but offers no liability protection.

Chapter 1 presents the three major categories of business entities and explores how each is formed and what their specific advantages and disadvantages are.

 # Chapter 2—Torts

Litigation falls into one of two major categories: criminal or civil. This text does not deal with criminal litigation. Civil litigation can be further divided into two classifications: torts and breach of contract. A lawsuit that is centered around a party's failure to perform in accordance with an agreement is a breach of contract action. Any other legal disagreement that is not a breach of contract is classified as a tort.

Torts apparently encompass a wide variety of legal problems. The most common type of tort in the construction industry is negligence, although other types do occur.

A tort has been committed when a person has a legal duty to do something and then fails to comply with this duty. Chapter 2 provides a broad overview of the various types of torts, including intentional torts, negligence, and strict liability.

Chapter 3—Contracts

Even a small construction project can possibly have nearly one hundred contracts. The general contractor will have agreements with the owner, suppliers, and subcontractors. These contracts may be simple writings or even oral agreements. Because of the existence of these wide array of contracts, it is worthwhile to have a working knowledge of the law of contracts.

Chapter 3 provides an overview of the legal theory of a valid contract. A valid contract must have a valid offer, acceptance, and be supported by consideration by both parties. Examples of these three items are presented as well as defenses to enforcement of a valid contract.

Chapter 4— Uniform Commercial Code

The Uniform Commercial Code (U.C.C.) provides a standard set of rules used in lieu of the usual law of contracts when the sale of goods are involved. The U.C.C. rules apply only to the sale of goods and does not cover the sale of services. Based on this distinction, it would appear that the U.C.C. would seldom apply to the construction industry, but this is not the case because courts have allowed U.C.C. principles to be applied by analogy to construction cases.

Chapter 4 presents some of the rules of interest provided by the U.C.C.

Chapter 5—Case law

Chapter 5 presents a discussion of eleven actual cases that centered on construction issues. These cases offer some interesting insight into lawsuits involving torts, contracts, and warranties.

Chapter 6—Construction contracts

The American Institute of Architects (AIA) has developed standard contracts that are widely used for construction projects, where the parties merely fill in the blanks in the preprinted forms. Unfortunately these standard contracts are not adaptable to residential construction projects. For residential construction, the contractor will typically use a contract obtained from another contractor or will have a lawyer draft a standard contract. Because the contract will be used numerous times, it would be foolish not to have a complete understanding of each and every item.

Chapter 6 discusses the various clauses that appear in residential construction contracts. A sample contract is provided in Appendix A.

 # Chapter 7—Specifications

The construction contract lists the documents that the contractor must be in compliance with. The design drawings typically lead the list of documents. These drawings provide the necessary dimensions, member sizes, as well as other essential information. But even the most detailed drawings cannot list all the information to construct a building. This is the reason why design drawings need to be supplemented with specifications.

Specifications are written instructions that provide detailed information on products, material, and performance requirements. Since the specifications become part of the contract by reference, their importance cannot be overstated. Chapter 7 provides an overview of the information typically provided in a set of specifications. A sample set of specifications is provided in Appendix B.

 # Chapter 8—Subcontractor contracts

Subcontractors will contract directly with the general contractor. On large projects, these contracts can be in excess of one hundred pages. In contrast, the contracts with subcontractors for residential projects rarely exceed one page.

The wisdom of using such a sparse contract is questionable at best, and the general contractor should consider using a more detailed agreement. Chapter 8 is devoted to presenting topics that should be addressed in a detailed contract between the general contractor and a subcontractor.

Chapter 9—Safety

The most important part of any construction project is safety. Failure to keep an accident-free worksite invites financial disaster for everyone involved.

In the 1970s, the Federal government enacted the Occupational Safety and Health Act to provide a safe working environment for employees. These rules cover a wide variety of requirements for many different industries. Part 1926 is applicable specifically to the construction industry, and Chapter 9 covers the applicable rules from Part 1926.

Chapter 10—Mechanic's liens

Mechanic's liens are a set of rules that assist the contractor in obtaining payment for labor, material and services—accomplished by allowing the contractor to "lien the property" of the owner for an amount equal to the enhancement of the property from the construction. Chapter 10 discusses the nuances of the mechanic's lien laws.

Chapter 11—Arbitration

Litigation costs are a direct drain on the profits of the contractor, as well as the owner. Regardless of who wins the judgment in the court battle, there seldom is a clear-cut winner. For this reason, litigation should be avoided at all costs.

If the parties are unable to reach a settlement to their dispute, litigation is the usual course of action. An alternative to this course is arbitration: an arrangement whereby both parties can tell their side of the story to a neutral party, and where both parties agree to abide by the decision of this neutral party. This method of dispute resolution can be both cheaper and more expedient than traditional litigation.

Parties are free to set up the rules for conducting the arbitration. Standard sets of rules can be obtained from arbitration services or nonprofit organizations specializing in arbitration, to avoid having to prepare this complex set of rules. As an example, the American Arbitration Association (AAA) provides "Construction Industry Arbitration Rules" to parties desiring to settle construction disputes. Read Chapter 11 for the specifics.

Chapter 12—Pretrial litigation

It is not uncommon for contractors to find themselves in the position of defending a lawsuit. To minimize damage, it is important for the contractor to take an active role in the legal process.

The majority of lawsuits (well over 90%) are settled some time before trial begins. The time leading up to the start of trial is called pretrial. Chapter 12 discusses pretrial issues including the selection of an attorney, legal documents initiating the lawsuit, and information gathering.

Chapter 13—Trial

If all negotiations have failed, a disagreement may likely proceed to trial. Chapter 13 discusses the various phases of a trial. Also discussed in this chapter is what evidence will be allowed at trial.

Chapter 14—Property

A construction project may die a slow death while the contractor tries to obtain a zoning change. A contractor should be knowledgeable in land zoning when building an entire subdivision, when the project is conditioned on a zoning change, or when the contractor is purchasing a parcel of land and selling the house and land as one package. This chapter explores various land zoning issues, as well as various issues related to property.

Appendix A

Appendix A provides a sample construction contract for residential construction.

Appendix B

Appendix B provides a sample set of specifications for residential construction.

Appendix C

Appendix C provides a reprint of the Construction Industry Arbitration Rules as provided by the American Arbitration Association.

These chapters and appendices are written to assist the contractor in understanding the legal system. However, you should understand that this book is not a substitute for legal counsel. The differences in the legal aptitude needed for avoiding legal problems and handling legal problems is significant, and this book should only be used for the purpose of avoiding common legal problems and understanding the problems that occur. Again, do not consider this book as a substitute for competent legal counsel.

1

Corporations, partnerships, & sole proprietorships

One of the first legal issues to confront the aspiring homebuilder is deciding what form to operate the business. The construction company can be conducted as a corporation, a partnership, a sole proprietorship, or a hybrid of these options, and the form of business chosen will directly impact the owner's liability exposure and the amount of accounting work required, as well as have income tax ramifications. Haphazardly choosing to start a business without proper planning in this area can result in financial losses to the entrepreneur far in excess of the initial investment.

This chapter will present the three major categories of business entities, describe how these entities are formed, and explain each one's advantages and disadvantages.

Sole proprietorship

A *sole proprietorship* is a business where one individual personally owns all of the assets of the business. No formal formation requirements are necessary to become a sole proprietor.

Starting a sole proprietorship takes limited resources and effort. One merely begins the business; no legal documents need be prepared, nor any government forms filed. Annual paperwork necessary for other forms of business is avoided, and extra tax return preparation work is minimized.

The simplicity of operating as a sole proprietorship is overshadowed by one major disadvantage: a sole proprietor takes full responsibility for all liabilities of the business. Because the sole proprietor *is* the business, the corresponding debts and liabilities follow. The sole proprietor is personally liable for any negligent act or breach of contract of the company. Creditors can seek reimbursement from the personal assets of the general contractor. One must clearly understand that the personal assets of the general contractor operating as a sole proprietor are always at risk.

 # Corporation

In contrast, the corporation is the opposite in regards to advantages and disadvantages. A corporation is an artificially created entity developed to allow a business to have an identity that is separate from the owners. For where, in a sole proprietorship, the identity of the business and the owner are one and the same, in a corporation the business and owner are two separate and distinct identities. Because of this split personality arrangement, the owners can have a financial interest in a business without personal liability exposure. The only assets at risk are the assets of the corporation.

The benefits gained by being a corporation come at a price. Both initial and maintenance costs are higher for a corporation, and the corporation will also be subject to taxation of profit above and beyond what the individual owner pays.

Corporate status is given by individual states and not by the United States government. Although corporate status will have a direct bearing on taxes paid to the federal government, the federal government has no direct involvement in the forming or maintaining of corporate status. Therefore, if for some reason a business desires corporate status in all fifty states, then the business would need to incorporate in each of the fifty states. However, corporate status in one state for the most part is recognized in the other forty-nine states. An out-of-state corporation (called a *foreign corporation*) may not be able to conduct business without some type of permission from the appropriate state.

Corporate status is achieved by filing the necessary paperwork—called the "Articles of Incorporation." This paperwork requires that the business requesting corporate status provide pertinent information about the business such as

➤ type of business.

➤ official company name.

➤ location of offices.

If the Articles of Incorporation are correctly filed and the appropriate fees are paid, the state will grant corporate status. Receiving corporate status is in itself not enough to be provided with reduced liability benefits. The corporation must operate properly to maintain corporate status. In particular, the corporation must keep its identity separate from that of the owners (called *shareholders*). If the identity of the corporation cannot be distinguished from the identity of the owners, the liability protection given by the corporate status will fail. In legal terms, this is termed the "piercing of the corporate veil."

Keeping the corporate identity separate from that of the shareholders is not difficult. Corporate property should be held in the name of the corporation. Corporate bank accounts should also be held in the name of the corporation and should under no circumstances be intermingled with the personal assets of the owners. All contracts, purchasers, and agreements should clearly designate that business is being done in the name and interest of the corporation. Using a common-sense approach to maintaining the individuality of the corporation, as well as proper submission of the government required annual paperwork, will allow one to enjoy corporate status.

As previously noted, corporations are taxed as an individual entity. In most cases, the owner is in essence paying double taxes—once for the profits of the corporation and once for the personal profits realized from the corporation. It would be wise to discuss the ramifications with a tax advisor prior to setting up a corporation. No general statement can be made because each person's financial position is unique when considering taxes.

One method of avoiding some of the problems of being a corporation is to set up the business as a specific type of corporation called an *S-corporation*. S-corporation status is available to a company with a small amount of shareholders. S-corporations do not pay corporate tax; rather, the profit is added directly to the taxable income of the shareholders. The S-corporation must be treated with an identity of its own just like a regular corporation.

Another variation of the corporate status is the *closely held corporation*. A closely held corporation usually has one or very few shareholders who typically manage the business. Closely held corporations have restrictions on the sale of shares. For instance, the rules of a closely held corporation might require that the stock in the corporation can only be sold to existing stockholders. This type of arrangement ensures that the corporation will continue to be run by a tight-knit group of investors (often family members).

The corporation is given its existence by the state through the Articles of Incorporation. However, rules on how the shareholders will run the business are not provided by the state but by the corporate bylaws. These bylaws lay out the rules that the shareholders will abide by; they also provide other information such as this:

➢ Directors: How many directors will be elected, and how they will be elected; how vacancies will be filled; and the meeting times of the board of directors.

➢ Officers: How officers will be chosen or removed, and how the officers will handle day to day operations.

➢ Shareholder meetings: Where and when they will be held; how shareholders will be notified of meetings; and how many are needed for a quorum.

 # Partnership

The final category of a business is the partnership. A *partnership* is where two or more people agree to carry out, as joint owners, a business venture to benefit the joint owners. That is, the owners (or partners) work for the benefits of the partnerships and not for their own individual gain.

A partnership is formed when the partners agree to work together for the common goal of the business. The agreement to work together can be expressed (in writing) or it may be implied by the conduct of the partners. A partnership has the same advantages as the sole proprietorship in that it can be started with little effort and minimal formalities.

The disadvantages of the partnership are similar to, if not worse than, that of the sole proprietorship. Partners are liable for the actions of themselves as well as all of the other partners. If one partner breaches a contract that was signed in the name of the partnership, the other partners' personal assets can be confiscated to pay the resulting damages. The debts and liabilities of the partnership are also personal debts of each and every partner.

As previously noted, there are no formal requirements to form a partnership. It can be difficult at times to determine if individuals are existing as sole proprietors working together or as a partnership. The latter case may be undesirable since individuals would be liable for the actions of the other individuals. The courts will look at the following to determine if there is indeed a partnership:

➤ Are individuals sharing gross returns?

➤ Are individuals sharing losses and profits?

➤ How is title to property being held?

➤ What name is being used for the business?

No one item from this list will of itself determine if a partnership exists. If individuals do not want to be treated as a partnership, their actions should clearly reflect that position.

If a partnership does exist, then each partner owes the other partners a fiduciary duty. Partners must work for the common good and not personal gain at the expense of the partners. If an opportunity arises that would be an appropriate venture for the partnership, an individual cannot secretly partake in the venture. A fiduciary duty would require that the partner offer the opportunity to the partnership first.

There is a special type of member of a partnership called a *limited partner* (often also called a *silent partner*). The limited partner contributes capital to the partnership venture but does not participate in the day-to-day activities of the business. This type of partner is acting solely as an investor, and accordingly the law typically limits liability to the amount of money invested. The limited partner still maintains the majority of a full partner's rights, including the right to vote on partnership issues, getting a share of the profits, and being allowed to inspect the financial records. However, the name of the limited partner cannot be used in the company name.

When setting up a partnership, a contract between the prospective partners should be written to address, as a minimum, the following items:

> ➤ Initial financial contribution of each partner.

> ➤ When and how profits will be divided.

> ➤ How losses will be divided.

> ➤ Duties of each partner.

> ➤ How the partnership will handle the addition of new partners, and the death or retirement of existing partners.

> ➤ How financial records will be kept and their availability to all partners.

> ➤ Location and name of business.

> ➤ The date the partnership will officially begin as well as end.

 # Summary

The personal assets of a sole proprietor are always at risk to satisfy debts of the business.

Sole proprietorships require the least amount of start-up effort from a business formation viewpoint.

The formation of a corporation requires the filing of the "Articles of Incorporation" with the appropriate state agency.

The owners of the corporation must agree on a set of rules for operating the business. These rules are called *bylaws*.

The corporation has an identity separate from the identity of its owners. For this reason, corporate finances, bank accounts as well as all other transactions, must not be commingled with that of the owners.

If a corporation is properly organized and maintained, the owners' personal assets are not at risk.

A partnership is formed when two or more people are working together for the common good of the business.

Partners are personally liable for any debts incurred by other partners acting in the name of the partnership.

The personal assets of the partners are always at risk to satisfy debts of the partnership.

There need not be a written agreement to have a partnership. A partnership can be implied by the actions of the individuals.

A limited partner invests in the partnership but is not involved in the day-to-day operations.

A limited partner is only liable up to the amount of the money invested in the partnership.

Torts

Civil lawsuits can be divided into two different categories: torts and breach of contract. A lawsuit that centers around a party's failure to perform in accordance with an agreement is a *breach of contract*. All other civil actions that do not qualify as a breach of contract fall into a catch-all category called *torts*. It is easy to see that this category of lawsuits will consist of a wide variety of legal actions.

Although there are many types of torts, this text will be limited to discussion of the following four groups:

➤ Intentional torts against the person

➤ Intentional torts against property

➤ Negligence

➤ Strict tort liability

Negligence is the most common form of tort litigation in the construction industry. Nevertheless, it is important to have an understanding of other torts to obtain a more complete knowledge of negligence. Intentional torts, though not common to the construction industry, will be covered as well simply to provide completeness.

This chapter will provide a broad overview of the various types of torts, while Chapter 5 will present actual tort cases in the construction industry.

It is important at this juncture to note that the torts presented in this chapter are discussed in a civil action context as opposed to a criminal action. In some instances, the two could overlap: for example, intentionally striking a person would give rise to legal actions for both criminal and civil assault. A criminal proceeding can only be brought by the government because the government is responsible for upholding the laws and punishing violators, while civil actions are brought by injured persons to receive payment for damages. This text only deals with civil actions.

A tort has been committed when a person has a legal duty to do something or to refrain from doing something and the person has failed to comply with this duty. The first group of torts to be covered is intentional torts against the person.

Intentional torts against the person

Intentional torts against the person can be subdivided into the following types:

➤ Assault

➤ Battery

➤ False imprisonment

Assault

The media has so often connected the words assault and battery that it leaves one with the impression that the two are really one action. The term "assault" itself has often been misused in that it is thought to be some type of offensive contact. In actuality, an assault has been committed if the following are satisfied:

➤ A person (called a *tortfeasor*) intends to put another person (the victim) in apprehension of a harmful or offensive contact.

➤ The victim is aware of and experiences the resulting apprehension.

The two key words in these two requirements are "intends" and "apprehension." To have the required intent, the tortfeasor must have a desire to cause the consequences of his act. Furthermore, the victim must experience apprehension from the action. The supersensitive person will not be considered assaulted if a reasonable person would not have felt apprehension from the alleged assault. The following examples illustrate the requirements of the intentional tort of assault.

Example 1: Assault

Jean, the county building inspector, refuses to issue an occupancy permit for a structure built by ABC Contractors. While Jean inspects the first floor, ABC's foreman, Ty, drops a pencil from the second story directly in front of Jean, not hitting her. Ty does not intend to hit Jean, only to startle her, and he successfully accomplishes that purpose. Is Ty liable for assault?

Yes. The elements of assault have been satisfied. Ty had intent and he put Jean into a state of apprehension.

Example 2: Assault

Isaac and Gina are employed by XYZ Paving. Isaac is irritated by Gina's continued refusal to repay a gambling debt owed to him. During lunch break, while Gina is taking a nap, Isaac starts a steamroller, floors the accelerator, and heads directly for Gina. Isaac has no intention of hitting Gina but passes within an inch of her feet. Having had a busy morning, Gina never wakes up and is unaware of the incident. Can Gina sue Isaac for assault when she is later told of the incident?

No. Gina was asleep and unaware of the situation she was in, which means she never experienced apprehension. The same conclusion would be reached if Gina were awake and facing the opposite direction and thus didn't notice the incident.

Example 3: Assault

Gus, a crane operator, is a decorated veteran of several wars. But as a result of his tour of duties, he has developed psychological problems. Greg repairs cranes for Gus's company and thinks it would be comical if he adjusted the crane engine to have backfire multiple times during operation. When Gus uses the crane the following day, it backfires and he recalls some very unpleasant war memories. He is so shaken by the experience that he can no longer work the remainder of the day. Has Greg committed an assault against Gus?

Probably not. Because Greg did not know of Gus's mental problems, he lacked the requisite intent needed to commit an assault. But if Greg *had* known of the mental problems of Gus, it would probably be considered an assault.

📜 Battery

A battery differs from an assault in that a battery requires an offensive contact with the person. Note that the word "offensive" is used rather than "physical." A battery can occur if something is connected to the person (for example, knocking a person's hat off her head).

The elements that form the intentional tort of battery are as follows:

> ➤ A tortfeasor intends to cause a harmful contact or an assault.

> ➤ The action has resulted in an offensive contact.

A battery, as was discussed for the intentional tort of assault, requires that there be some intent. If for example, a person tripped over a curb and grabbed onto a passerby to keep from falling, there is lack of intent and thus no battery has been committed. Note that a battery does not have the requirement that the victim be aware of the incident.

The following examples illustrate the requirements of the intentional tort of battery.

Example 4: Battery

Consider the same scenario as Example 1, in which Ty drops a pencil from the second floor directly over the building inspector—except that in this case, Ty wants to, and does, hit Jean on the toe. Is Ty liable for battery by hitting someone on the toe with a pencil?

Yes. The requirements for battery were satisfied because intent was coupled with an offensive contact.

Example 5: Battery

Consider the same scenario as Example 2, in which Isaac races a steamroller towards Gina. Unfortunately for Gina, Isaac misjudges his driving capabilities and runs over Gina's thumbnail. Isaac feels terrible about the incident because he had no intention of hitting Gina. Has Isaac committed a battery?

Yes. One form of a battery is when a person desires to cause apprehension in a person and the action accidentally results in offensive contact. It is irrelevant that Isaac did not want to hit Gina.

Example 6: Battery

Consider the same scenario as Example 3, in which Isaac is irritated at Gina and races a steamroller towards her. Isaac would enjoy rolling over Gina, but she wakes up and jumps out of the way. Unfortunately, Isaac cannot stop the steamroller and hits poor Jack, who was directly behind Gina. Has Isaac committed a battery against Jack even though he had no intention of hitting him?

Yes. Even though Isaac did not have the intent to hit Jack, he still has committed a battery. Under the doctrine of "transferred intent," if the tortfeasor desires to make offensive contact with one person and accidentally hits another person, a battery has been committed.

 # False imprisonment

The final intentional torts to the person that will be discussed is false imprisonment. The elements of false imprisonment are as follows:

➤ The tortfeasor intends to confine a person within certain boundaries.

➤ The person is directly or indirectly confined.

➤ The person is conscious of their imprisonment.

At first impression, it appears that it would be fairly simple to determine if a person has been falsely imprisoned. However, this is not always the case. It is often difficult to determine what actually qualifies as confinement, because physical barriers are not the only means of confinement. In some cases, threats of force could be enough to provide the necessary confinement. The following examples illustrate the intentional tort of false imprisonment.

Example 7: False imprisonment

Tommasina is a painter for ABC Painting. Michele insists that Tommasina complete the painting of the interior of the house prior to leaving for the day, but Tommasina refuses to comply. While Tommasina is changing her clothes, Michele manages to take and hide them. Michele then tells Tommasina that she will return her clothes when Tommasina has finished painting the interior of the house. Is Michele guilty of the intentional tort of false imprisonment?

Yes. The taking of Tommasina's clothes results in her direct confinement, because she is unable to leave the premises.

Example 8: False imprisonment

Antonio is an engineer with Fast Engineering. Bianca, the chief engineer, wants Antonio to complete the project he is working on by the end of the day, so she quietly locks Antonio inside his office and disconnects the telephone. Antonio is hard at work and never notices that he is trapped in his office. But before he finds out, Bianca reconnects the phone and unlocks the door. Can Antonio sue Bianca for the intentional tort of false imprisonment?

No. One of the elements of false imprisonment is that the victims be aware that they are confined. Because Antonio is too busy working to know of his confinement, he will not be able to maintain a false imprisonment action.

Intentional torts against property

Intentional torts do not necessarily need to be involved with a human being. The ownership of property comes with certain rights of exclusive use of that property. The intentional interference with these rights can be an intentional tort. The intentional torts against property that will be discussed are

> ➤ Trespass to land.

> ➤ Trespass to chattel.

> ➤ Conversion.

A *trespass to land* has occurred when there is an intentional uninvited entry onto the land of another. Two of the words in this definition require further definition. First, although intent is needed, an entry is a trespass regardless of whether the entry was in error (i.e., person was under assumption that property is owned by someone else). Also, the term "land" includes the property that is located below the ground surface, as well as some of the air space above the property. The measurement of a "reasonable distance" is used for the protected zone both above and below the property. It is considered a trespass below the ground if the work (i.e., mining) detrimentally affects the property above. For air space, it is a trespass if the action is such that the landowner's enjoyment and use of the land is disturbed.

Example 9: Trespass

Tony, a carpenter, is nailing down floor joists to the sill plate. One of his hammer swings goes astray and sends the nail flying into the neighbor's vegetable garden. Can the neighbor sue Tony for trespass to land?

No. Trespass to land is an intentional tort, and one of the requirements for trespass is that the action be intentional. Tony had no intention of sending the nail flying into the neighbor's garden.

Example 10: Trespass

Ines is using a bulldozer to strip the topsoil on a lot located at the top of a hill. In the process of grading, the brakes fail and the bulldozer begins a rapid travel down the hill. Ines realizes that her only chance of survival is to slam into some nearby trees, so she does so and ends up causing damage to several of them. The neighbor sues Ines both for trespass and to recover the value of the damaged trees. Will the neighbor prevail?

Yes and no. Ines was in a very serious predicament that was life-threatening both for her and others; because it was an emergency, her action is not considered a trespass. But even though Ines did not trespass, it does not relieve her of her obligation to pay for the damage she caused to the trees.

Trespass to chattel, & conversion

The remaining two types of intentional torts to property—trespass to chattels and conversion—are sometimes very similar since both involve loss of the use of property. *Chattel* is a term used by the legal profession to denote an article of personal property. Trespass to chattels is an act by someone that takes the article of personal property away from the rightful owner on a temporary basis. The elements that compose an action of trespass to chattel are as follows:

> ➤ The tortfeasor interferes temporarily with the owner's right of possession of the property.

> ➤ The owner has suffered some amount of damage as a result.

The intentional tort of conversion of property is an action whereby the article of personal property is permanently taken away from the rightful owner. The elements that compose an action of conversion are as follows:

> ➤ The tortfeasor intentionally interferes with the owner's rights of the possession of property.

> ➤ The damages are such that it would only be fair to give the injured party full compensation for the property.

Comparison of a conversion with trespass to chattel shows that the difference is really a matter of degree. When the loss of ownership of a piece of property has been violated to the extent that full compensation should be given to the owner, the act changes from a trespass to conversion.

Example 11: Trespass to chattel

Amy steals a welding torch from Peter Construction Rentals. A week later, Peter locates Amy and reclaims his property. Has Amy committed the intentional tort of trespass to chattel?

Yes. Peter would be able to collect a week of rentals from Amy.

Example 12: Trespass to chattel, & conversion

Take the same facts as Example 11, except that Amy also steals the portable gas tanks that are needed to utilize the torch. When Peter eventually finds his equipment, the gas tanks are empty. Under what theory can Peter sue?

Both trespass to chattel and conversion. The trespass to chattel suit would be used as presented in the previous example. Amy would also be liable for conversion because she used the gas.

Negligence

Up to this point, the discussion has been focused solely on intentional torts. But by far, the most common type of tort in construction is negligence.

Often it is difficult to distinguish between an intentional tort and negligence. An intentional tort is an act that is wrong as a matter of law, whereas negligent acts are acts that are typically within the law but make the tortfeasor liable for not exercising the proper degree of care. In other words, the intentional tort is an act inconsistent with the law, while the negligent action is not in conflict with the laws but is in conflict with the proper way of conducting oneself.

The elements that comprise a negligence action are

> ➤ the breach of a duty.

> ➤ the breach caused the problem.

> ➤ the problem resulted in damages.

Each and every entity has a duty to exercise some level of care to all who may be foreseeably injured by their actions. This statement has two key terms that need to be addressed: level of care, and foreseeability.

Some type of measuring stick is needed to determine what level of care must be provided. Courts utilize what is called the "reasonable person" standard. This standard requires that a level of care be exercised that is equal to what would be provided by the reasonable person in a similar situation. It can be seen that this standard is sometimes difficult to precisely define and leads to a wide variety of judicial interpretations.

The level of care that must be provided by a professional is higher than that of the ordinary person. A contractor is expected to possess the knowledge of a member of his profession in the same locale, who is in good standing. The reasonable man standard is not used for contractors since contractors are expected to perform at this higher level of competence.

Example 13: Negligence

Blase is welding a splice plate onto a bridge girder above a street. While working one day, a welding spark goes astray and ignites an automobile directly adjacent to the bridge. The car explodes. Has Blase breached his duty of care?

Yes. If the reasonable person standard is applied, he has breached his duty of care by operating a welding torch in an unsafe condition. If a higher standard of care were applied, this decision is even easier because a welder in good standing in any locale would be cognizant of the danger of welding near automobiles.

Example 14: Negligence

Jonathan, a licensed architect, designs a house in 1994 to be built in City A. In 1995 an earthquake levels the house. In the early 1990s, the local association of architects had provided seminars on earthquake design. In these seminars, they discussed the possibility of earthquakes in City A. Jonathan claims that, because 99.9% of the public would not have known about the earthquake potential, he is not negligent. Is Jonathan correct?

No. Professionals are not measured by the reasonable person standard but rather by the knowledge of a local professional in good standing. It is irrelevant that most of the public is unaware of the possibility of earthquakes; the professional must provide a higher level of care. Because there were classes on earthquakes, it is obvious that Jonathan should have recognized the possibility of earthquakes.

Besides the level of care that must be provided, foreseeability is also an issue when considering a breach of duty. A duty of care is owed to all foreseeable persons. Who is considered foreseeable is difficult to define and must be decided on a case-by-case basis. The following example will help illustrate the extent of what is considered foreseeable.

Example 15: Negligence

Take the same facts as Example 15. Resulting from the burning automobile, an explosion shatters windows of a nearby building. Glass from the shattered window injures Briana. Will Briana win a suit against Blase for negligence?

Yes. Blase should be well aware that his failure to contain his welding sparks can lead to fire and explosions. It is foreseeable that explosions can break windows and cause injury.

The next consideration after proving that the tortfeasor had a duty and breached that duty, is that the breach caused the problem in question. The following examples show that causation may be difficult to establish.

Example 16: Negligence

Dan is attaching shingles to the roof of a two-story structure. Because he tends to be lazy, Dan is carelessly tossing the excess shingles from the roof rather than cautiously dropping them. One of the errant shingles hits Anna and injures her eye while she is driving by the remodeling project. Has Dan's actions caused the physical damage to Anna?

Yes. It is obvious that Dan's action caused this problem.

Example 17: Negligence

After Anna is hit by the shingle in the previous example, she loses control of the car, runs up on the curb, and hits Dominic, who is raking leaves in front of his house. Can Dominic sue Dan for his actions?

Yes. Dominic's injuries are directly caused by Dan's actions.

Example 18: Negligence

After being hit by the car, Dominic is rushed to the hospital. There it is decided that Dominic needs surgery on his leg. Kyle, the hospital's surgeon, performs the operation but is unsuccessful in saving the use of Dominic's leg, leaving him crippled. It is later discovered that Kyle performed the operation in a negligent manner. Will Dominic be successful in his lawsuit for negligence against Dan?

Maybe. If the surgeon is negligent, Dan will not be liable for Dominic becoming crippled because Dan did not cause this problem. However, if Dominic would have been crippled regardless of the operation's success, Dan will be liable for this portion of the damages.

The final element of the tort of negligence is the establishment of damages. It is not enough that the injured party can prove the tortfeasor had a duty, breached that duty, and the injury occurred because of the breach. If damages cannot be established, the plaintiff will receive nothing. The concept of damages itself is not difficult to grasp, but proving the exact damages may be difficult because damages can be physical as well as economic. It is not unusual to have a trial where the defendant has admitted negligence but where the damages flowing from this negligence are in question.

Up to this point the elements of what constitutes negligence have been discussed. Other important issues relating to negligence are

➤ vicarious liability.

➤ assumption of the risk.

➤ landowner responsibility.

What follows is a brief introduction to these negligence-related topics.

Vicarious liability

A tort committed by an employee may result in the employer being held liable for the resulting damages. The binding of the employer by the actions of the employee is called *vicarious liability*.

An employer will only be held liable if the employee was acting within the scope of their duties of employment when the tort occurred. A slight detour from the employee's assigned duties will not relieve the employer of liability. If the employee has gone beyond a slight detour of his or her duty (an act called a *frolic*), it could relieve the employer of liability. There is a fine line between what is considered a detour (for example, doing more work than the company has authorized) and what is a frolic (for example, using a company truck to move personal belongings).

For the most part, an employer can only be held liable for the torts of employees and not workers employed by others. When a general contractor hires subcontractors, the former is not necessarily liable for the latter. For this reason, it is important that the general contractor not hold itself out as the employer of the subcontractor because liability from the actions of the subcontractor could attach to the general contractor.

The general contractor will be held liable for the acts of the subcontractor for what is classified as extremely hazardous waste (one such example being dynamite blasting). The laws do not allow for the general contractor to put all the liability on a subcontractor; this is a matter of public policy because it would allow for a great deal of sham arrangements to avoid lawsuits and responsibility.

Although an employer may be held liable for the negligence of employees, this will not be the case for intentional torts. Assault, battery, and false imprisonment are considered similar to frolics and relieve the employer of liability.

Example 19: Vicarious liability

Kelvin is president of ABC Blasting. He is hired to blast a tunnel through a mountain so that a road can be constructed through it. Kelvin hires Alyssia, a dynamite expert of XYZ Company, to do the work. Alyssia overestimates the amount of dynamite needed and levels a nearby town, so the residents of the town sue Kelvin for negligence. Kelvin requests that the case against him be dismissed because he was not the negligent party. Will he prevail?

No. A general contractor is not necessarily liable for the negligence of a subcontractor. But because this project consists of a very dangerous activity, the general rule is inapplicable and Kelvin is liable for Alyssia's negligence.

 # Assumption of the risk

A person may be relieved of negligent liability if the injured party assumed the risk. A party has assumed the risk if they are aware of the danger and proceed knowing of these dangers. If for some reason a party has no alternative but to proceed it is not considered assumption of the risk.

Example 20: Assumption of the risk

Tammy, the foreman of ABC Company, is in charge of constructing a 99-story apartment complex. Access to the top floor is provided by a construction elevator. Anthony is a welder for ABC Company; he knows that Tammy is not safety-conscious and has never had the construction elevator inspected as required by the city code. Anthony is nervous about using the elevator but does so anyway because the alternative is to spend two hours walking the stairs. One day after completing his shift, Anthony uses the elevator to get down from the 99th floor. During his descent, the elevator cable snaps, and he is severely injured. Anthony sues Tammy for negligence, but Tammy defends herself on the grounds that Anthony knew the elevator was probably not operating properly and therefore assumed the risk. Will Tammy prevail?

No. Although Anthony may have indeed assumed the risk, Tammy cannot use this as a defense because there was really no other realistic means of coming down from the building.

Landowner responsibility

In the previous comments about negligence, we saw that one of the required elements is duty. For a landowner to be negligent, it must be shown that a duty of care was to be provided by the landowner. Whether a duty of care is owed to persons on a piece of property is dependent on the status of the person. It also depends on whether the injury was caused by natural conditions or artificial conditions created by changes to the property.

In regards to natural conditions, a landowner has no duty of care with respect to the property unless the person was invited onto the property. For artificially created conditions, the landowner has some level of duty to anyone that has entered the property, but no duty to undiscovered trespassers.

Strict tort liability

The final area of torts that will be discussed is strict tort liability (products liability), which allows for the recovery of damages for injuries suffered from a product that is sold to consumers. In other words, a person can recover damages when they are injured by a product.

At first, products liability would not seem to apply to construction, but if you consider all of the products used in construction, the relevance of products liability becomes more apparent. Furthermore, courts often compare a house to a product and thus use product liability laws.

Understanding products liability is best explained by comparing it to a negligence action. Both causes of action are based on a duty, breach of duty, causation, and damages. The difference is that, for products liability actions, the "reasonable man" standard is not applicable. Rather, both the requirement of duty and breach of duty are satisfied just by showing that the supplied product was defective. This lessens the requirement that the plaintiff needs to establish to win the case. Rather than showing what a "reasonable man" would do, the product simply has to be shown to be defective.

(Note that the magnitude of research testing, studies, or time spent on making the product safe is irrelevant. The standard that others use in the industry is also irrelevant. All that is of interest is whether or not the product is defective.)

The court's theory on lessening the burden on the plaintiff is one of economics. It is believed that a manufacturer can better shoulder the burden of the damages from a defective product than can a few injured consumers. The manufacturer can raise the price of the product a small percentage to cover the cost of injuries, and the manufacturer's market will remain relatively unchanged. In contrast, an injured consumer may be placed in a situation where he or she cannot work or even support his or her family.

In determining if the manufacturer is liable, the judge or jury will decide if the product was in a defective condition that made it unreasonably dangerous. They will not look at fault, but only at the condition of the product when it left the manufacturer's hands.

Strict liability in tort was developed to help protect consumers against defective products. In recent years, courts have allowed strict liability to extend beyond products and be utilized in service-type industries including construction.

 # Summary

Civil lawsuits are divided into two categories: torts and breach of contract.

Civil lawsuits are tort cases unless a contract is at issue.

Four types of torts are presented in this chapter: intentional torts against the person, intentional torts against property, negligence, and strict tort liability (products liability).

A person who has committed a tort is called a *tortfeasor*.

In some cases, a tort can subject the tortfeasor to both civil and criminal action.

Three types of intentional torts against the person were presented in this chapter: assault, battery, and false imprisonment.

The intentional tort of assault has been committed when a tortfeasor intends to put another person in apprehension of a harmful or offensive contact, and the victim is aware of and experiences the resulting apprehension.

The intentional tort of battery has been committed when a tortfeasor intends to cause a harmful contact or an assault and the action resulted in harmful contact.

Note that there is no assault or battery unless the person intended to cause the offensive action.

If the tortfeasor desires to make offensive contact with one person and accidentally makes it with another person, a battery has been committed under the doctrine of *transferred intent*.

The elements of false imprisonment are that the tortfeasor intends to confine a person within certain boundaries, the person is directly or indirectly confined, and the person is conscious of their imprisonment.

Three types of intentional torts against property were covered in this chapter: trespass to land, trespass to chattel, and conversion.

A trespass to land has occurred when there is an intentional uninvited entry onto the land of another.

The rights of land ownership allow for some rights of the property above and below ground.

Work below ground that detrimentally affects the property above ground is considered a trespass.

Air travel is a trespass if it disturbs the landowner's enjoyment and use of the property.

A trespass to chattel occurs when the tortfeasor intentionally interferes temporarily with the owner's right of possession of the property and the owner has suffered some amount of damages as a result.

A conversion occurs when the tortfeasor intentionally interferes with the rights of the owner to possession of the property and damages are such that it would only be fair to give the injured party full compensation for the property.

Trespass to chattel and conversion differ only in the degree of the violation of the property.

Intentional torts are wrong as a matter of law, while negligent actions are within the law but fail to exercise a duty of care.

A negligence action is comprised of a breach of duty, that breach causing a problem, and that problem resulting in damages.

Courts utilize the measure of what a "reasonable person" would do to determine the level of duty of care required.

The duty of care that must be provided by professionals is higher than that of the "reasonable person." Professionals must provide a level of care that is equal or greater than that of a good standing member of the same profession in the same locale.

A duty of care is owed to all people that are foreseeably affected by the action of the alleged negligent person.

A plaintiff must show that there was actual damages to receive money under a negligence theory.

A tort committed by an employee may result in the employer being held liable under the theory of *vicarious liability*.

A tortfeasor might be relieved of liability if the plaintiff was aware of the danger and proceeded despite the dangers.

A property owner has a duty to keep their land safe. The level of duty required depends on whether the injured person is a trespasser or was invited on the property. Also, it depends on whether the problem was created by a natural condition or man-made hazard (artificially created).

Strict tort liability allows for the recovery of damages for injuries suffered from a product sold to consumers.

A strict tort legal action has similar requirements to a negligence action, except that you need only show that the product was defective in lieu of showing duty and breach of duty.

3

Contracts

Agreeing to the terms of a contract is typically considered to be a significant event. But if we review our daily activity, we'll see that we enter into a multitude of contracts every day. When we purchase supplies from a hardware store, we are executing a contract with the owner; the owner agrees to provide a product that meets a certain standard, while we agree to compensate the owner. When we desire to have material delivered to the job site, we pay a predetermined amount of money, and the delivery company agrees to transport the material safely to the job site. We often proceed through our daily activities, giving little thought to the fact that we are indeed entering into binding contracts. At some point, though, a contract becomes important enough to warrant a more cautious approach before we accept its terms.

Many times, the construction contract is signed prior to the start of construction and is given little attention until a dispute erupts between the parties. At that point, the parties will desperately review the terms of the contract in an attempt to support their position. In many cases, the contract is poorly drafted, which forces the parties to litigate in order to interpret the precise meaning of the contract. A well-drafted contract avoids this situation.

There is an important distinction in contract law between the rules of the sale of goods as opposed to nongoods (services). The sale of goods are typically covered by the rules of the Uniform Commercial Code, which can significantly differ from the rules for sales of nongood items.

This chapter will present the fundamentals of contract law. Chapter 4 will discuss contracts for the sale of goods and warranties, while Chapter 6 will discuss contracts specific to the residential construction industry. A sample contract (for reference purposes only) is provided in Appendix A.

We typically think of contracts as valid only if there is an express agreement, typically in writing, by all the parties involved, but those that are simply implied may also be valid and binding. To define the two, then, an *express contract* is an agreement where the terms are clearly stated orally or in writing, while an *implied contract* is not evidenced by an oral or written agreement but rather is implied by law based on the surrounding circumstances.

Example 3-1: Express contract

Lisa, the vice president of ABC Builders, has an oral agreement with John from XYZ Fences to construct a fence around a construction zone. The contract is never put into writing, although they have an oral agreement in regards to all the issues. After John has received the specially ordered fencing material, Lisa decides she no longer wants the fence. Is Lisa in breach of contract?

Yes. Lisa has breached an express contract. Oral contracts are express contracts and are binding on the parties.

Example 3-2: Implied contract

Gus, president of M and D Decorators, agrees to paint the exterior of a house at 111 Main Street. Gus inadvertently shows up at the wrong house at 111 Maple Street. Gina, the owner of the house is aware that Gus is at the wrong address. She lets him proceed in the hopes of getting a free paint job. When Gus finishes, Gina refuses to pay because she thinks she does not have a contract for painting services. Will Gus prevail if he brings suit against Gina for breach of contract?

Yes. Even though Gus does not have an express contract with Gina, he will still recover for his services. Gina's failure to stop him when she knew of his mistake gives rise to an implied contract for his painting services.

When determining whether there is a valid contract or not, the following items are examined:

➢ Was consideration given by both parties?

➢ Was there a valid offer?

➢ Was there a valid acceptance?

➢ Are there any valid defenses to the contract?

The first requirement (consideration) provides that all parties to the contract must be giving up something of value for the contract to be enforceable. The item of value is called consideration. Consideration can be in any number of forms; money, property, and providing services are samples of what qualifies as consideration.

Example 3-3: Consideration

Jean signs a contract with Greg to purchase a piece of property owned by Greg. Jean agrees to paint Greg's house in exchange for the property. Does Jean's offer to exchange services for property satisfy consideration agreement?

Yes. Jean is giving up something of value, her painting services, in exchange for the property. Giving up something of value satisfies consideration requirements.

Failure to provide consideration, and the resulting unenforceable contract, commonly occurs when gifts are involved. A promise to make a gift will not usually be enforced since the receiver of the gift is not providing consideration in exchange for the gift.

Example 3-4: Consideration

Tony, a remodeling contractor, signs a contract to add an attached garage to Michele's house. Tony has made an incredible profit on this project because weather conditions were unusually favorable. Near the end of the project, Michele asks Tony to repair a crack in the concrete slab in the basement. Tony agrees to do it in the following month but never does return. Will Michele win a suit to have Tony do this repair?

No. Tony's offer was merely gratuitous. Because Michele provided no consideration for Tony's promise, he is not bound to do the work. Note that it is irrelevant that Tony made a hefty profit on the project because that contract is unrelated to the crack repair.

A promise to make a gift can be enforced as a contract if the promise caused a detrimental reliance. If a person relies on a promise to the extent that it places them in a bad position that would not have occurred but for the promise, the promise may be enforced as a contract.

Example 3-5: Consideration

Isaac is a painter for ABC Painting. His Uncle Chuck, a self-made millionaire, does not like the fact that Isaac works so hard to make ends meet. Uncle Chuck tells Isaac that if he quits work, he will give him money for living expenses while Isaac pursues a college degree. Based on this promise, Isaac quits his job, but Uncle Chuck never gives Isaac any money. Isaac desperately tries to get his painting job back to no avail and remains unemployed for six months. Can Isaac sue Uncle Chuck for breach of contract for his failure to follow through with the gift?

Yes. Promises to make gifts are usually unenforceable contracts. However, if the receiver relies on the promise to his detriment, it may be enforceable. Isaac would probably be entitled to damages from his Uncle for his lost wages for the time he was unemployed.

Nominal consideration will not suffice to make a contract enforceable. Courts looking at the exchange of valuable consideration for a nominal amount realize that the arrangement is probably a sham.

Example 3-6: Consideration

Peter wants to give his Porsche to his brother-in-law Jack because he is extremely fond of him. Peter has made this promise several times in the past but has never followed through on his promises. Jack realizes that Peter's promise was always unenforceable for lack of consideration on his part. This time when Peter makes his promise, Jack gives Peter 10 dollars. Later when Peter does not give Jack the Porsche, Jack files suit against Peter for breach of contract. Will Jack prevail?

No. Jack has not given any valuable consideration and therefore the promise is unenforceable. The 10 dollars that Jack gave to Peter is nominal and does not qualify as consideration.

Past consideration is not sufficient to make a contract enforceable. The agreed-upon consideration must be exchanged at the time the promise is made.

Example 3-7: Consideration

Jonathan is excited that his high-rise construction project finished on schedule. To show his gratitude for the extra hours that his employees have voluntarily worked, he promises to buy them all new cars. But he never follows through on his promise to give the employees new cars. Will the employees be successful in a breach of contract lawsuit?

No. The extra hours worked by the employees is past consideration and therefore the contract is unenforceable. Remember, as previously discussed, that the promise may be enforceable if an employee relied on this promise to their detriment.

The second element essential to an enforceable contract is a *valid offer*. To have a valid offer, there must be an expression of intent by the offerer that communicates the essential terms of the offer to the other party (offeree). If a person jokingly makes an offer, it would not be an enforceable contract because there is a lack of intent to enter into a contract. A court must look at the circumstances as well as the language used to determine if there is the intent to make an offer.

An additional aspect to consider when investigating if an offer is binding is whether the language is an actual offer or just an offer to negotiate. Acceptance of the latter will not bind the offerer.

Example 3-8: Offer

Briana, a senior partner in an engineering firm, contacts Amy of XYZ Contractors with the following letter:

"Would you be interested in utilizing our site inspection services for a $10,000 a month fee?"

Is this considered an offer such that Amy can accept the terms, thereby binding Briana?

Probably not. When correspondence utilizes phrases such as "Would you consider . . .?" or "Would you be interested . . .?" or similar terms, it is considered to be negotiations. When more definite terms such as "I am offering . . ." or "Our asking price is . . ." are used, there is greater evidence of intent and the correspondence is considered a valid offer.

An offer must contain essential terms to be valid, and these terms are dependent on the type of contract at issue. The typical essential terms are the names of the contracting parties, identification of the subject matter of the contract, price, when performance is required, etc.

For a valid offer to be binding, there must be an acceptance before the offer has terminated. If the proposed offer contains a time limit in which the offer must be accepted, this is a simple matter. But when there is no date of termination listed in the offer, the court will use a "reasonable time" to determine if the offer was timely accepted. An offerer can revoke an offer any time prior to acceptance.

Example 3-9: Revoke of offer

Dan, a general contractor, sends out the following letter to other local builders:

"I am asking $7000 for all concrete formwork I presently have in stock. Call me if you are interested."

Kyle gets the letter and decides he would be interested in purchasing the formwork. Before he responds, Dan calls him and states that he is no longer interested in selling the formwork. Can Kyle force Dan to sell the formwork?

No. An offer can be revoked at any time before it is accepted.

Example 3-10: Revoke of offer

Use the same facts as Example 3-9, except that the letter includes the following:

"I will hold this price open for two weeks from the date of this letter."

Dan calls Kyle and tells him that he is no longer selling the formwork. Can Kyle force Dan to sell him the formwork?

No. Even though Dan has agreed to keep the offer open for two weeks, he can still revoke the offer since Kyle never accepted. The result would be different if Kyle had told Dan he was undecided and gave $20 to keep the offer available. In this case, Kyle would have what is called an *option* and Dan would be unable to revoke the offer until the agreed-upon time period expired.

The third requirement needed to have an enforceable contract is a valid acceptance of the offer. A *valid acceptance* consists of a communication to the offerer that all the terms of the contract are acceptable. A valid acceptance can only be made by the person the offer was directed to.

An acceptance must be expressly communicated to the offerer; silence or a failure to act by the person is not an acceptance. This rule prevents offerers from unfairly binding the receiver of an offer. However, there are circumstances where silence will be considered an acceptance of an offer, based on past dealings between the parties, the custom of the industry, and the facts surrounding negotiations.

If an acceptance is conditioned on terms not provided, it is not a valid acceptance. This rule is called the *mirror image* rule. Under this rule, an acceptance is valid only if it is an acceptance of the exact terms of the offer. Any deviation in terms from the original offer effectively make the alleged acceptance a counteroffer and *not* an acceptance.

Example 3-11: Mirror image

Kelvin, a carpet installer, sends an offer to carpet a home being built by ABC Builders. The offer states that Kelvin can complete the work within 14 days of starting the work. Lore, the superintendent for ABC Builders, sends a response to Kelvin stating that the terms are acceptable but that the work must be completed within seven days. Is Lore's response a valid acceptance?

No. Lore can only accept the terms that were offered by Kelvin. Lore's change in the time allowed for installation changes her response from an acceptance to a counteroffer.

Even if the conditions of consideration, offer, and acceptance are satisfied, there may be valid defenses that may make the contract unenforceable. Some of the defenses to the enforcement of an otherwise valid contract are

> ➤ a lack of capacity.

> ➤ a mistake.

> ➤ fraud.

> illegality.

> unconscionability.

> a statute of fraud.

Unenforceable contracts that involve lack of capacity are of three types:

> Minors

> Mental incompetence

> Under the influence of drugs or alcohol

A minor is not liable for contracts entered into except for the purchase of necessities. When a minor contracts for food, shelter, clothing or similar necessities, the minor is liable under the terms of the contract. A minor has the power to void any contract that is not for necessities. However, the other party to the contract cannot void the contract and must fulfill the terms of the contract if the minor decides to enforce it. One can easily see the difficulties that can develop when contracting with a minor.

Lack of mental capacity is similar to contracting with a minor. If a person is of a condition that they lack the understanding of the nature of the transaction, then they may void the contract at their discretion. Similar to contracts with minors, the party contracting with a person that lacks mental capacity cannot void the contract.

The final type of person who lacks the capacity to contract are those under the influence of alcohol or drugs. A person under the influence can have a contract voided if they can prove that because of the alcohol or drugs they could not understand what they were doing.

The next method by which an otherwise valid contract can become unenforceable is in the case of a mistake. Mistakes can be either unilateral or mutual.

A mutual mistake is one that is made by both parties. When both parties have made a mistake, the contract is voidable by the party that is affected adversely by the mistake.

Example 3-12: Mistake

Vincenza, the owner of a small piece of valuable property, leases the property to Nick so that he can build bins to store harvested grain products. Nick's building plans are rejected by the local building department. The rejection has occurred because zoning laws forbid any structure 20 feet or taller in this area. Can Nick have the lease voided because of the mutual mistake?

Yes. The basic assumption of fact was that the grain silos could be constructed on the leased property. Because both parties were mistaken, the party suffering a detriment from the mistake has the option of voiding the contract.

There is a distinction between a mistake in judgment and a mistake in fact. A mistake in judgment (i.e., Nick believes the project will make money) is different than a mistake in fact (i.e., structure could not legally be built). A mistake in judgment will not allow for voiding the contract.

The other type of mistake is a mistake by only one of the contracting parties (called a *unilateral mistake*). The term "mistake" in this contract applies to items that are computational in nature as opposed to mistakes in judgment. Once again, a mistake in judgment is not sufficient to void a contract.

If the nonmistaken party is aware that the other party is mistaken, then the contract can be voided. Voiding of the contract would not prevent the nonmistaken party from receiving some payment of damages resulting from the voiding of the contract. If both parties are unaware of the mistake, then the contract is not void unless the terms are so unfair that it would be totally unjust to enforce it.

Example 3-13: Mistake

Dominic desires to have his doctor's office remodeled. He has an architect prepare drawings and specifications and puts the project out to bid to three contractors. Anthony submits his bid in the amount of $10,000. Unfortunately, two drawings are stuck together and Anthony is unaware that a special structural support is needed for an

X-ray machine to be included in the remodeling. The two other contractors submit bids in excess of $40,000. Dominic immediately writes a letter of acceptance to Anthony. When Anthony discovers his mistake, he refuses to do any work on the project. Can Dominic force Anthony to do the work?

No. When Dominic received the bids he was on notice that there was some type of error in Anthony's bid as evidenced by the disparity in the bids. It was obvious that Anthony made a computational error.

Contracts entered into using misrepresentations are voidable by the party that was defrauded. Misrepresentation, also called fraud, occurs when the defendant causes someone else to act upon wrong information and this person does indeed rely on the misrepresentation to their detriment. The defendant must be aware that their behavior is a false misrepresentation.

Example 3-14: Fraud

Tammy is a contractor with minimal ethics. Tammy contacts Antonella—a homeowner—and fraudulently represents that the basement is filled with radon gas. Tammy offers to fix the alleged emergency problem by putting in an additional layer of concrete at the cost of $40,000. Antonella is concerned with the health of her children and signs the contract offered by Tammy. But prior to the start of work, Antonella finds out there is no radon in her house. Can Antonella be forced to pay money for the work agreed to in the contract?

No. This contract was obtained under false pretenses. The contract can thus be voided by the person who was defrauded.

As a matter of public policy, contracts that are illegal are unenforceable. The courts have no interest in enforcing contracts that involve unethical behavior. The question of illegality that may arise in construction is the issue of licensing requirements.

Example 3-15: Illegal

Gina is the owner of ABC Engineers, a company not registered to practice engineering in State X. Lisa hires Gina to design a residential structure. When one-third of the design is finished, Lisa decides that Gina's work is completely substandard. Lisa terminates Gina's services and refuses to pay any of the bill. Gina files suit for breach of contract. Lisa defends by claiming that Gina is not entitled to any money because her firm is not licensed as required by the State of X. Will Lisa prevail?

Probably. Gina's failure to be a properly registered engineering company would make the contract illegal and unenforceable.

Just as courts will not enforce contracts that are illegal, they will not enforce contracts that are grossly unfair. A grossly unfair contract (called an *unconscionable contract*) is a contract that is so one-sided it would be unjust to enforce it.

Example 3-16: Unconscionable

John sells magazines door to door. Archie agrees to purchase a one-year subscription for a construction magazine. Archie signs the contract for the subscription. One of the terms of the contract is "If Archie fails to make a payment, he agrees to pay $2000 in damages."

Archie misses the second payment and John files suit to obtain the $2000 for breach of contract. Will John prevail?

No. Even though the contract is valid, the court will not enforce it because the damage remedy is so drastic.

Unconscionability also arises in the contract of exculpatory clauses. An exculpatory clause is a portion of a contract that relieves a party of liability for his negligence. It is difficult to give a general answer when an exculpatory clause will be found unconscionable.

Example 3-17: Exculpatory clause

Gus would like Mike of ABC Contractors to build a fishing pond on his property. Mike is concerned that if there is a major rainstorm, the pond may overflow and damage neighboring property. Gus agrees to pay any and all claims arising out of such an accident, under the condition that Mike reduce his price by $10,000. The agreement is in writing and signed by both parties. Is the contract unconscionable due to the presence of language that excuses Mike's negligent behavior?

Probably not. True, courts will not allow a party to be relieved from liability from their own negligence. If Mike cannot build the pond properly, he should be liable for his negligence. However, courts will overlook this situation if the person has bargained for the benefit of this clause.

The final form of defense against an otherwise valid contract is those contracts that fall under the statute of frauds. The statute of frauds (not to be confused with fraud in general) was taken from the laws of England as are a great majority of our laws. The law was developed to prevent perjury in certain types of legal circumstances. The statute of fraud requires that certain contracts be in writing if the contracts are to be enforceable. The types of contracts that fall under the statute of frauds are

➤ marriage.

➤ those that will take longer than one year to perform.

➤ land sale.

➤ sale of goods greater than $500.

➤ bonding and insurance.

Any of these types of contracts must be in writing if they are to be enforceable. The written contract must include the following:

➤ Identity of the parties

➤ Description of the subject matter of the contract

➤ Signature of the party accused of breach of contract

Example 3-18: Statute of frauds

Ines is interested in purchasing a piece of property owned by Steve. Steve drafts a contract, signs it, and has it sent to Ines. Ines subsequently has an emergency meeting that requires her to leave the state. Prior to her departure, she stops by Steve's house. Steve is having breakfast with several of the local church pastors. Ines clearly states to the entire crowd that she wants to purchase the property and that Steve should set up arrangements for transfer of the property. When Ines gets back from her trip, she is not interested in the property and refuses to follow through on the deal. Steve files suit to force Ines to buy the land and intends to use the local pastors as witnesses. Will Steve prevail?

No. The sale of land falls under the statute of frauds. The statute of fraud requires that contracts be in writing and at least be signed by the party in breach. Because Ines did not sign the contract, it does not matter what she said to Steve, the contract is not binding.

If there is indeed a contract and there are no valid defenses, the plaintiff is entitled to damages. Damages fall generally into three categories:

➢ Compensatory

➢ Nominal damages

➢ Punitive damages

Compensatory damages provide money to the injured party to place them in a position they would have been in had there been no breach. Nominal damages are given when the plaintiff is the prevailing party but is only entitled to a small sum of money. Such a small damage award is appropriate where there has been an injury to the plaintiff but the plaintiff has suffered minimal harm.

A type of damage that is not at all related to damages suffered by the plaintiff is punitive damages. Punitive damages are awarded by judges who feel that merely paying the prevailing parity is insufficient to deter the defendant's conduct in the future. The purpose is not only to reprimand the defendant, but also to provide a disincentive for others to act in a similar manner.

In construction cases, when the owner breaches a contract, the builder is entitled to recover profits plus the money expended on the project. When the contractor breaches, the owner is entitled to recover the costs necessary to complete the project.

An injured party may not be interested in obtaining damages but rather desire that the terms of the contract be fulfilled. When the injured party is requesting that the other party fulfill the terms of the contract, the injured party is requesting "specific performance." Specific performance is allowed when the courts feel that damages may not be adequate compensation.

Courts will usually not utilize specific performance in construction cases due to the difficult nature of making sure the construction is of proper quality.

 # Summary

Contract rules are different for the sale of goods as opposed to the sale of items that are not goods (i.e., services).

An express contract is an agreement where the terms are clearly stated orally or in writing.

An implied contract is not evidenced by an oral or written agreement but rather is implied by law based on the surrounding circumstances.

The following must be looked at to determine if a contract is valid or not: consideration, valid offer, valid acceptance, and valid defenses.

The requirement of consideration provides that all parties to a contract must be giving up something of value.

Failure to provide consideration, and the resulting unenforceable contract, commonly occur when gifts are involved.

A promise to make a gift can be enforced as a contract if the promise caused a detrimental reliance.

Something of a nominal value given for consideration will not suffice to make a contract enforceable.

Past consideration is not sufficient to make a contract enforceable.

A valid offer must be an expression of intent by the offerer that communicates the essential terms to the other party.

An aspect to consider when investigating if an offer is binding is whether the language is an actual offer or just an offer to negotiate.

An offer must contain essential terms to be valid. Essential terms of a contract are dependent on the type of contract at issue.

For a valid offer to be binding, there must be an acceptance before the offer has terminated.

A valid acceptance consists of a communication to the offerer that all the terms are acceptable.

Even if the offer and acceptance requirements of a contract are satisfied, there may be valid defenses that make the contract unenforceable.

Some defenses to an otherwise valid contract are a lack of capacity, a mistake, fraud, illegality, unconscionability, and statute of fraud.

A minor is not liable for contracts entered into except for the purchase of necessities.

A person under the influence of drugs or alcohol can have a contract voided if they can prove because of their condition they could not understand what they were doing.

A mistake in judgment is different than a mistake in fact. A mistake in judgment will not allow for voiding the contract.

Contracts entered into using misrepresentation are voidable by the party that was defrauded.

As a matter of public policy, contracts that are illegal are unenforceable.

Just as courts will not enforce contracts that are illegal, they will not enforce contracts that are grossly unfair.

The statute of frauds requires that certain contracts be in writing if the contracts are to be enforceable.

Contracts that are under the statute of frauds are marriage, contracts that will take longer than one year to enforce, land sales, sales of goods over $500, and bonding and insurance agreements.

Compensatory damages provide money to the injured party to place them in a position that would have been attained had there been no breach.

Nominal damages are given when the plaintiff has prevailed in court but shown no actual damages.

Punitive damages are awarded by judges who feel that merely paying the prevailing party is not sufficient to deter the defendant's conduct in the future.

4

Uniform Commercial Code

The Uniform Commercial Code (U.C.C.) provides a standard set of rules for handling transactions in the commercial setting. These standard sets of rules adopted a great deal of the existing judicial opinions on contract law (called *common law*) but also have some notable differences. The U.C.C. rules are available to be adopted in full or in a modified form by any of the states. With the exception of the state of Louisiana, every other state has adopted the U.C.C.

Some of the commercial transactions that are covered by the U.C.C. include the sale of goods, investment securities, and secured transactions; however, the U.C.C. does not apply to services. Therefore, it would appear that the U.C.C. would be limited in the construction industry to disputes with suppliers. But this is not the case because courts often allow U.C.C. principles to be applied by analogy to construction cases, which leaves the contractor possibly subject to a different set of legal rules and the accompanying results if the U.C.C. is applied.

The chapters that compose the U.C.C. are as follows:

Article 1:   General Provisions
Article 2:   Sales
Article 2A: Leases
Article 3:   Negotiable Instruments
Article 4:   Bank Deposits and Collections
Article 4A: Funds Transfers
Article 5:   Letters of Credits
Article 6:   (Revised) Bulk Sales
Article 7:   Warehouse Receipts, Bills of Lading and Other
                  Documents of Title
Article 8:   Investment Securities
Article 9:   Secured Transactions; Sales of Accounts
Article 10: Effective Date and Repealer
Article 11: Effective Date and Transition Provisions

The article of interest for the construction industry is #2: Sales. Covered here from that article, under the title of "Firm Offer," is the following:

➤ Additional Terms in the Acceptance

➤ Modification of the Contract without Consideration

➤ Implied Warranty of Merchantability

➤ Implied Warranty of Fitness for a Particular Purpose

➤ Exclusion of Warranties

You should note that the U.C.C. sometimes differentiates between merchants and nonmerchants. A merchant is a person who regularly deals with or has special knowledge of the goods of the kind being sold. Consider this example.

Example 4-1: Merchant vs. nonmerchant

Jean, the president of a cement manufacturing company, has decided that it's time to replace all of the office equipment. Isaac is interested in purchasing the old equipment from Jean's company. They both agree to a price, but right before the transaction date Jean decides she will not sell the old equipment. Isaac believes that they have a contract and Jean has breached it. Can Isaac file suit against Jean's company for violation of the U.C.C. rules?

Probably. Because the problem centers around the sale of goods, the U.C.C. is applicable. But portions of the U.C.C. are applicable only against those who are merchants. Although a cement manufacturer is a merchant with respect to cement sales, they are not a merchant with respect to the sale of office equipment. Only the portion of the U.C.C. rules that are applicable to nonmerchants can be utilized against Jean's company.

Firm offer

As we learned in the contract chapter, an offer can be withdrawn at any time before it has been accepted. An offer must only be held open for a person who has given consideration for that right. Money may be paid to the person making the offer to induce them to keep the availability of the offer open for a set amount of time, and this offer cannot be withdrawn until the agreed-upon time frame has expired because consideration was paid for that right.

The U.C.C. rules differ from the common law approach just described, according to Article 2.2.5 (Firm Offers), which states that

> . . . an offer by a merchant to buy or sell goods in a signed writing which by its terms give assurance that it will be held open is not revocable, for lack of consideration, during the time stated or if no time is stated for a reasonable time, but in no event may such period of irrevocability exceed three months, but any such term of assurance on a form supplied by the offeree must be separately signed by the offeror.

The important elements of this rule are that

➤ the person must be a merchant.

➤ the offer must be in a signed writing.

➤ the offer must state that it will be held open.

➤ the period of irrevocability cannot exceed three months.

If these elements are satisfied, then no consideration need be paid to the person making the offer to keep it open for the stated time.

Example 4-2: Firm offer

Gina, a salesperson with ABC Nuts and Bolts, sends a letter to Gus to offer him a sale price on aluminum bolts if he responds within 10 days. The day after Gus receives the offer, he writes a letter to Gina accepting the offer. Just as Gus is about to put the acceptance letter in the mail, he receives a telephone call from Gina who tells him she will not honor the price quoted in her offer. Gus still wants the bolts at the price quoted and files suit to recover damages. Will Gus prevail?

Yes. ABC Nuts and Bolts is a merchant who sent a signed offer stating that they would offer the price for 10 days; therefore the offer cannot be revoked. As noted earlier, the answer is different if the traditional laws of contracts are used.

Additional terms in the acceptance

Prior to the existence of uniform commercial codes, courts followed the "mirror image" rules, which requires that the acceptance could only be exactly what was offered. If the acceptance deviated from what was offered, then it was considered a counteroffer and *not* an acceptance. The U.C.C. does not utilize the mirror image rule, as can be seen in the text of 2-207.

> 1. A definite and seasonable expression of acceptance or a written confirmation which is sent within a reasonable time operates as an acceptance even though it states terms additional to or different from those offered or agreed upon, unless acceptance is expressly made conditional on assent to the additional or different terms.
>
> 2. The additional terms are to be construed as proposals for addition to the contract. Between merchants such terms become part of the contract unless:
>   a. the offer expressly limits acceptance to the terms of the offer;
>   b. they materially alter it; or
>   c. notification of objection to them has already been given or is given within a reasonable time after notice of them is received.

Part 2 provides that an acceptance that does not mirror image the offer is not a counteroffer but rather is considered a contract with proposed changes. This applies only to nonmerchants. For merchants, the deviations from the offer become part of the contract unless the offer prohibited it, the change materially alters the contract, and the person who made the offer does not object in a timely fashion. For a clearer understanding, compare and contrast the next three examples.

Example 4-3: Additional terms in the acceptance

Peter finds some ceramic tile in his garage while doing his spring cleaning. Peter sends a brief note to his neighbor, Amy, offering to sell her the tile for $1000. Amy responds with a note that states "I will be happy to purchase the tile at the stated price, and I want you to buff each piece and call me, and I will pick them up." Do Amy and Peter have a contract under the rules of the U.C.C?

Yes. Amy has agreed to the offer and there is a contract. However, because Peter is not a merchant, he is not required to buff the tile.

Example 4-4: Additional terms in the acceptance

Use the same facts as Example 4-3, except that this time Amy's response is "I will agree to purchase the tile at the stated price provided you will buff each piece." Is there a contract under the rules of the U.C.C?

No. The terminology used by Amy in her response does not qualify as an acceptance. It is a counteroffer.

Example 4-5: Additional terms in the acceptance

Use the same fact as Example 4-3, except that Peter and Amy are both merchants in the tile industry. Is there a contract under the U.C.C?

Yes. Not only is there a contract, but if Peter does not object in a timely manner, the buffing request becomes part of the terms of the contract.

Modifications of the contract without consideration

Under the common law, a contract must be supported by consideration by all parties to the contract (see preceding chapter). If one party does not give consideration, the transaction will be treated as a gift rather than as a contractual obligation.

The same principles are applicable to modifications to a contract. If one party voluntarily modifies the contract and the other party pays no consideration for the modification, it is not enforceable.

The U.C.C. takes a different position on modifications to contracts in Article 2-209.

> 1. An agreement modifying a contract within this Article needs no consideration to be binding.

Example 4-6: Contract modification

ABC Lumber agrees to provide 10-foot-long 2 × 4s at a price of $4 each for a period of twelve months to XYZ Builders. Six months into the contract, the price of wood has tripled. ABC sends a letter to XYZ Builders asking for a modification in the price of the studs from $4 to $10. XYZ agrees to the modification. Several months later XYZ refuses to pay the additional costs. Was the modification binding on XYZ Builders?

Yes. Because the contract was for the sale of goods, the U.C.C. is applicable. Section 2-209 provides that a modification to a contract does not require consideration. Note that if the U.C.C. was not utilized, the modification would not be binding on XYZ Builders and ABC Lumber would be required to furnish the studs at the original contract price.

Implied warranty of merchantability

The seller of goods may provide the purchaser with a written warranty. In the absence of a written warranty, the purchaser has little recourse under the common law. The U.C.C. provides the purchaser of goods with an implied warranty regardless of whether there is any written or other express warranties. Section 2-314 provides an implied warranty of merchantability as follows:

1. Unless excluded or modified, a warranty that the goods shall be merchantable is implied in a contract for their sale if the seller is a merchant with respect to goods of that kind. Under this section, the serving for value of food or drink to be consumed either on the premises or elsewhere is a sale.

2. Goods to be merchantable must be at least such as
   a. pass without objection in the trade under the contract description
   b. in the case of fungible goods, are of fair average quality without the description
   c. are fit for the ordinary purposes for which such goods are used
   d. run within the variations permitted by the agreement, of even kind, quality and quantity within each unit and among all units involved
   e. are adequately contained, packaged, and labeled as the agreement may require
   f. conform to the promise or affirmations of fact made on the containment or label, if any.

Under the requirements of this implied warranty, as applied to the construction industry, the goods must pass without objection in the trade and be fit for the ordinary purpose of which the goods are used.

Example 4-7: Implied warranty of merchantability

Red Construction Company purchases a gross of nails from Blue Supply Company. Blue Supply does not provide any written warranties for this product. During construction Red Construction finds that the tops of nearly one-half of the nails break when hit with a hammer. Red Construction Company files suit to obtain reimbursement of one-half of the cost of the nails. Blue Supply Company defends on the grounds that there was no warranty provided. Will Blue Supply prevail?

No. Even though there is no express warranty, the U.C.C. provides the purchaser with an implied warranty of merchantability, which requires that goods must pass without objection in the trade. Obviously, having one-half of the nail heads break off during use would not pass in the industry without objection.

Implied warranty of fitness for a particular purpose

Another implied warranty provided by the U.C.C. is located in Section 2-315 (Implied Warranty of Fitness for a Particular Purpose):

> Where the seller at the time of contracting has reason to know any particular purpose for which the goods are required and that the buyer is relying on the seller's skill or judgment to select or furnish suitable goods, there is unless excluded or modified an implied warranty that the goods shall be fit for such purpose.

The elements that need to be satisfied to utilize this warranty against a seller, merchant, or nonmerchant are as follows:

➤ The seller must know the purpose for which the goods will be used.

➤ The buyer must be relying on the judgment and skills of the seller.

The following example illustrates the application of this warranty.

Example 4-8: Implied warranty of fitness for a particular purpose

Antonio designs and constructs a grain storage silo for Dan. During the first windstorm, the grain silo collapses. Dan sues Antonio under the theory of an implied warranty of fitness for a particular purpose. Will Dan prevail?

Maybe. Courts have allowed structures such as grain silos to be subject to the rules of the U.C.C. by treating the structure similar to goods. In this case, the plaintiff will be allowed to collect damages if the buyer relied on the skill of the seller and the seller knew the purpose the silo would be used for.

Exclusion of warranties

The U.C.C. allows the seller to exclude all warranties including the two warranties previously discussed. However, any language excluding warranties must be plainly stated. Also, any disclaimer of the implied warranty of merchantability must contain the word "merchantability" to be effective.

Summary

The Uniform Commercial Code (U.C.C.) provides a standard set of rules for handling transactions in the commercial setting.

The U.C.C. has some notable differences as compared to the common law.

The U.C.C. applies to the sale of goods.

The U.C.C. does not apply to services rendered.

Courts have applied U.C.C. rules by analogy to the construction industry.

The rules provided by the U.C.C. sometimes distinguish between a merchant and a nonmerchant.

A firm offer may not be revoked under the U.C.C. even if no consideration was paid for that right.

Terms in the acceptance that differ from the terms of the offer may be included as part of the contract depending on whether the parties are merchants or not.

The U.C.C. allows a contract to be modified without consideration.

The U.C.C. provides an implied warranty of merchantability and an implied warranty of fitness for a particular use.

The seller may disclaim any implied warranties if it is noted in a conspicuous manner.

If the implied warranty of merchantability is disclaimed, the wording of the disclaimer must contain the word "merchantability."

5

Case law

The best way to learn something is to obtain hands-on experience. For example, if a contractor desired to get a better handle on costs and scheduling for masonry projects, his optimal learning process would include actual involvement at the site. This hands-on approach holds merit for a multitude of situations—but unfortunately the legal aspects of construction is not one of them. Participation in a lawsuit, either as plaintiff or defendant, usually does not lead to many pleasant memories.

The *preferred* method of learning about the legal side of construction is to review the lawsuits of others. This chapter presents eleven cases of interest to those in residential construction and will provide you with real-life applications of the principles presented in previous chapters.

You should understand that this chapter does not attempt to provide any current view of the law; the cases are only presented as to provide insight and provoke critical thinking on the subject. It is very possible that some of these cases have or will be subsequently overruled, but they were chosen because they were good examples for showing a broad overview of construction litigation. You should not rely on any of the cases presented herein as the current law but can use them as a starting point to obtain current case law.

In all cases presented, the losing party appealed the outcome. Many of these cases never went to trial because the judge believed that one of the parties' positions was in conflict with current law. Under these circumstances, the judge will dismiss the case prior to the start of a full trial. The losing party then has the option to appeal. If the appeal is successful, the higher court will instruct the lower court to change its decision and hear the entire case. If the losing party is unsuccessful with the appeal, the holding of the lower court is binding.

Here's a list of the cases discussed in this chapter, along with a basic description of each case's topic:

Case 1. Fisher v. Simon (1961) Supreme Court of Wisconsin: Can a person who purchased a home from a builder/seller sue for negligent construction for hidden defects?

Case 2. Navajo Circle v. Development Concepts (1979) Florida Court of Appeals: Is an architect required to provide a duty of care for persons that do not have a contract with the architect?

Case 3. Dow v. Holly Manufacturing (1958) Supreme Court of California: Can a general contractor be held liable for the negligent work of a subcontractor?

Case 4. Southern New England Telephone v. D'Addario Construction (1976) Supreme Court of Connecticut: Does the deviation from customary practice constitute negligence?

Case 5. Wendland v. Ridgefield Construction (1981) Supreme Court of Connecticut: If the contractor is in violation of an Occupational Safety and Health (OSHA) regulation, is the contractor negligent per se?

Case 6. Kenney v. Medlin Construction & Realty (1984) North Carolina Court of Appeals: What is the proper measure of damages for negligent construction?

Case 7. Barnes v. MacBrown & Company (1976) Supreme Court of Indiana: Can implied warranties provided by builder/seller apply to purchasers other than the original purchaser?

Case 8. Moxley v. Laramie Builders (1979) Supreme Court of Wyoming: Can implied warranties provided by a builder, who is not a seller, be used by subsequent purchasers?

Case 9. Terlinde v. Neely (1980) Supreme Court of South Carolina: Will a release of liability given by the original purchaser be binding for a subsequent purchaser?

Case 10. Kriegler v. Eichler Homes (1969) California Court of Appeals: Can the builder of mass-produced homes be held liable to a purchaser on the basis of strict liability for the failure of a heating system?

Case 11. Hyman v. Gordon (1973) California Court of Appeals: Can a builder be held liable to the purchaser on the basis of strict liability for improperly locating a water heater?

Let's look at each in detail.

Case 1

Can a person who purchased a home from a builder/seller sue for negligent construction for hidden defects?

Case name	Fisher vs. Simon
Decision date	December 29, 1961
Court	Supreme Court of Wisconsin
Case cite	112 N.W.2d 705
Plaintiff	Simon
Defendant	Fisher

❋ Prior holding

Small claims court of State of Wisconsin decided in favor of defendants that plaintiff failed to state facts sufficient to continue the case and judgment was entered dismissing the case.

❋ Facts

Fisher (defendant) built a single family residence in Wisconsin in 1958. Simon (plaintiff) entered into a contract with the defendant to purchase the house. The contract was not a construction contract but rather a real estate purchase agreement.

Cracks developed in the basement slab within one year of the purchase of the house. Widths of the cracks were of a magnitude that water penetrated into the basement. Subsequent investigation into the problem revealed that the backfill used at the basement walls contained pieces of timber and other debris, which allowed water to accumulate behind the walls and seep into the basement through the slab cracks. Repairs included removing the undesirable backfill and replacing it with proper material. The basement slab also was resurfaced.

The case was dismissed by the judge prior to being decided on the facts. The judge was of the opinion that a tort action was not maintainable under these facts.

✳ Plaintiff's position

One element of a tort action is the existence of a duty. A contractor has a duty to construct a building in a quality manner. The quality should be equal to that provided by a professional in good standing situated in the locale. A professional in good standing had a duty to provide a slab without excessive cracking, as well as a properly backfilled wall.

✳ Defendant's position

The defendant relied on previous court decisions that held that a builder who sells a completed house is not liable for undiscovered defects unless fraud was involved. In the defendant's opinion, if the court does not follow this viewpoint, contractors could be faced with liability many years after selling the house.

✳ Court's response

The court acknowledged that previous decisions held that a builder/seller could not be held liable for defects discovered after the property was sold. The reasoning behind these decisions was that public policy dictated that it would be unfair and unworkable to have a builder be subjected to liability long after losing control of the premises.

Despite the court's acknowledgment of these holdings, they reversed direction on their previous decisions. It was their opinion that public policy should be protecting the buyer from losses that result from negligent construction because the contractor is probably in a better financial position to remedy the defects. A builder/seller has a duty to construct a house without any hidden defects, and if the buyer can prove the remaining elements of a tort action, then damages should be recovered by the plaintiff.

✳ Court's decision

The plaintiff should be allowed to sue the defendant in tort. The case was sent back to the lower court to hear the case in accordance with tort law.

✳ Comments

Review of previous court decisions shows that the contractor could sell a house with hidden defects without liability. This same line of thinking was also used in the sale of existing homes and used cars. This "buyer beware" (*caveat emptor*) was prevalent in the ages prior to this suit. Since this time, the pendulum has swung to the opposite side and judges tend to bend over backwards to protect the consumer. This approach is evident when one looks at current standards, which require contractors to provide implied warranties, realtors and homeowners to disclose known defects, and lemon laws that protect the buyers of used automobiles.

✳ Referenced cases

Colton v. Foulkes 47 N.W.2d 901:Wisconsin

Guschl v. Schmidt 63 N.W.2d 759:Wisconsin

Colbert v. Holland Furnace 164 N.E.2d 162:Illinois

Levy v. Young Construction 139 A.2d 738:New Jersey

Combow v. Kansas City Ground 218 S.W.2d 539:Missouri

International Harvestor v. Sharoff 202 F.2d 52:Federal

Fentress v. Van Etta Motors 323 P.2d 227:California

Herme v. Tway 294 S.W.2d 534:Kentucky

Case 2

Is an architect required to provide a duty of care for persons that do not have a contract with the architect?

Case name	Navajo Circle v. Development Concepts & Others
Decision date	June 13, 1979
Court	Florida Court of Appeals
Case cite	373 So.2d 689
Plaintiff	Navajo Circle Condominium Association
Defendant	Fritzell Architects

❋ **Prior holding**
The trial court of the State of Florida granted motion of defendant for a dismissal of the case because the parties did not have a contract.

❋ **Facts**
A roof on a condominium was improperly constructed, resulting in the damage of some of the walls of the structure. Because of this damage, some of the condominiums were temporarily unleaseable.

Fritzell Architects (defendant) was hired to supervise both the original construction of the roofs as well as the subsequent repairs. The architects' contract was not with Navajo Circle (plaintiff), the condominium association.

Navajo Circle brought a negligence suit against Fritzell Architects. The lower court dismissed the case because it was of the opinion that there needed to be a contract between these two parties to maintain a negligence lawsuit.

❋ **Plaintiff's position**
The plaintiffs admitted that if they were suing under a contract theory, the case was properly dismissed. However, the plaintiffs argue that, because this is a tort action, no contractual relationship need exist. The issue in a negligence action is whether the defendant owed plaintiffs a duty and if the duty was breached. A contract may establish a duty, but its absence does not necessarily eliminate any duty of care.

❋ **Defendant's position**
Because there was no contract with the plaintiff, there was no duty owed to that party.

❋ **Court's response**
The Court's position was that, despite the judicial opinion some thirty years earlier, the Supreme Court was presently taking a broader view of the extension of tort liability. A recent Supreme

Court decision held that, where it is foreseeable that the plaintiff will suffer injury, the supplier of the service has a duty of care with respect to that plaintiff. An architect has a duty of care that requires the providing of a service that will not harm foreseeable persons.

✳ Court's decision

The plaintiff should be allowed to sue the defendant under a negligence theory despite the lack of a contractual relationship. The case was sent back to the lower courts for examination of the facts to determine if the architect was negligent.

✳ Comments

It is not uncommon in residential construction for the architect to have a contract with the builder rather than the buyer. Often the builder has a list of favorite architects and will present these plans to prospective buyers. If the plans are acceptable to the buyer, the builder will purchase the plans from the architect and pass the cost on to the purchaser.

✳ Referenced cases

Detweiler Bros. v. Graham 412 F.Supp 416:Federal

Cooper v. Juene 56 Cal.App3d 860:California

Meyer v. Graham 285 So.2d 397:Florida

Audlane Lumber v. Britt 168 So.2d 333:Florida

Geer v. Bennett 237 So.2d 311:Florida

Conklin v. Cohen 287 So.2d 56:Florida

Lemay v. U.S.H. Properties 338 So.2d 1143:Florida

Sickler v. Indian River Abstract 142 Fla.528:Florida

Simmons v. Owens 363 So.2d 142:Florida

Strathmore Condo Association v. Paver Development 369 So.2d 971:Florida

Case 3

Can a general contractor be held liable for the negligent work of a subcontractor?

Case name	Dow v. Holly Manufacturing & Others
Decision date	February 18, 1958
Court	Supreme Court of California
Case cite	321 P.2d 736
Plaintiff	Richard and Leona Dow
Defendant	George Bledsoe

✳ Prior holding

Plaintiffs were awarded damages by the jury against defendant for the wrongful deaths of the spouse and two children of the plaintiff.

✳ Facts

The general contractor (defendant) contracted with Buyer 1 to build a house. Buyer 1 sold the house to Buyer 2 before ever moving in. Within two years, Buyer 2 sold the house to Dow (plaintiff). Less than one year later, an adult and two children died from asphyxiation. The deaths were caused by the negligent installation of a defective heater. The subcontractor performed the heater installation.

Damages were awarded to the plaintiff from the general contractor. The general contractor appealed.

✳ Plaintiff's position

The general contractor has an overall responsibility for constructing a house with an adequate and safe heating system. Regardless of who installed the heating system, the general contractor is liable. The general contractor is responsible for ensuring that all work completed by the subcontractors was not performed in a negligent manner.

✳ Defendant's position

If the person who installed the heating system was an employee of the general contractor, then there would be liability. If the person who installed the heating system was a subcontractor, then the general contractor should not be liable.

✳ Court's response

The Court based its opinion on two points. First, the Court believed that, because the general contractor has full control of the project, then there must also be full responsibility for any problems that occur in regards to the project. The second point used by the court was an analogy between building construction and product liability. Building construction involves the purchase of—and assembly of—materials into a final product. This purchase and assembly scenario is similar to that used in other industries such as automobile manufacturing. In the case of automobile manufacturing, if a subcontractor negligently installed an engine part, the automobile manufacturer would be liable in tort. Likewise, a builder that utilizes a subcontractor that performs negligently should also be held liable.

✳ Court's decision

The Court upheld the decision of the lower court, which held that the general contractor was liable for the deaths of the occupants.

✳ Comments

The general contractor in this case tried to distinguish the heater installer as an independent subcontractor rather than an employee. The Supreme Court of California did not care which one of these two the installer was, because the general contractor was liable for the negligence of both.

There are situations where the classification of the person as either an employee, subcontractor, or independent is important. For example, the general contractor may have significantly less safety responsibility for independent contractors and subcontractors than for their own employees. This may also be of issue in large projects where it is difficult but important to determine the status of the negligent party and the corresponding duties and liabilities.

✳ **Referenced cases**

Brown v. Pepperdine Foundation 247 P.2d 352:California

Knell v. Morris 247 P.2d 352:California

Sayder v. Southern California Edition 285 P.2d 912:California

Slavin v. Leggett 177 A.120:New Jersey

Thornhill v. Carpenter Morton 108 N.E. 474:Massachusetts

Swift v. Hawkins 164 So.23:Mississippi

Moran v. Pittsburgh-Des Moines Steel 166 F.2d 908:Federal

Hunter v. Quality Homes 68 A.2d 620:Delaware

Coulton v. Foulkes 47 N.W.2d 901:Wisconsin

McCloud v. Levitt 79 F.Supp. 286:Federal

Inman v. Binghampton Housing Authority 152 N.Y.S.2d 79:New York

American Heating and Plumbing v. Grines:Mississippi

Gobrecht v. Beckwith 135 A.20:New Hampshire

 # Case 4

Does the deviation from customary practice constitute negligence?

Case name	Southern New England Telephone v. D'Addario Construction
Decision date	May 7, 1976
Court	Superior Court of Connecticut
Case cite	363 A.2d 766
Plaintiff	Southern New England Telephone Company
Defendant	D'Addario Construction Company

✳ **Prior holding**

Jury decided in favor of plaintiff that there was no negligence. Defendant requested that trial court set aside the jury verdict as not being supported by the evidence. The trial court of the sixth circuit of the State of Connecticut denied the motion.

✴ Facts

D'Addario (defendant) had a contract to install storm sewers in Bridgeport, Connecticut. An employee of the telephone company (plaintiff), who was present to protect the interests of his company, marked the location of a telephone line as being three feet to the side of a manhole. When one of D'Addario's employees lifted a manhole out of the ground with a backhoe, he damaged the buried telephone line. During the construction operations, the procedures prescribed by the telephone company for work in the area of their utility lines was not followed.

The jury in this case decided that D'Addario was not negligent. Southern New England Telephone appealed the decision.

✴ Plaintiff's position

The plaintiff claims that the decision by the jury should be changed because the jury unreasonably disregarded certain undisputed facts. In particular, their position was that the backhoe operator, D'Addario's employee, failed to follow the procedures outlined by the plaintiff. Because the defendant failed to follow this customary practice, the jury should have found the defendant guilty of negligence.

✴ Defendant's position

Defendant admits that they did not conform to the customary practice of the industry. However, failure to follow customary practice does not necessarily mean that a breach of duty occurred and there is no negligence.

✴ Court's response

The court's position is that there is no legal principle that states that nonconformance with customary practice is negligence. The custom of the industry is evidence that can be given to the jury, but it is not conclusive of negligence in and of itself. The jury heard the evidence and concluded that the defendant was not negligent. They obviously did not place as much weight on the fact that the defendant did not follow customary practice. This does not constitute any reversible error on the part of the jury.

✳ Court's decision
The jury deciding that the defendant was not negligent was not an unreasonable conclusion.

✳ Comments
This case falls into a category of the "negligence *per se*" cases. Negligence *per se* means that under certain circumstances a person is guilty as a matter of law and the element of duty and the breach of that duty need not be addressed. In this case, the plaintiff wanted the Court to take the position that failure to follow custom and standard practice in the industry was "negligence *per se*." The court did not follow this viewpoint.

✳ Referenced cases
Rood v. Russo 161 Conn.1:Connecticut

Martino v. Palladino 143 Conn. 547:Connecticut

Horvath v. Tontini 126 Conn. 462:Connecticut

Pappaleno v. Picknelly:135 Conn. 660

 # Case 5

If the contractor is in violation of an Occupational Safety and Health (OSHA) regulation, is the contractor negligent *per se*?

Case name	Wendland v. Ridgefield Construction
Decision date	May 12, 1981
Court	Supreme Court of Connecticut
Case cite	439 A.2d 954
Plaintiff	Alfred Wendland
Defendant	Ridgefield Construction Services

✳ Prior holding
Superior Court in the judicial district of Fairfield in the State of Connecticut using a jury ruled in favor of plaintiff in personal injury action.

❋ Facts

A general contractor was retained to do work at a high school. The general contractor hired Ridgefield Construction (defendant) as a subcontractor to perform excavation work. Ridgefield excavated the hole but did not properly shore it.

Carpenters were in the process of setting up the formwork for the concrete walls the day after a heavy rain. The trench collapsed while Wendland (plaintiff) was in the excavated area. The plaintiff suffered compound fractures in the leg. The plaintiff was not an employee of the defendant.

The Court instructed the jury that, if they found that the defendant violated OSHA regulations, then the defendant is negligent. The jury found that the defendant was negligent and gave a substantial damage award.

❋ Plaintiff's position

A violation of OSHA provisions is proof that the defendant is negligent. There is no need to show there was a duty and a breach of duty. The defendant dug the trench in violation of OSHA standards, the trench collapsed, injury occurred, and the defendant must be found negligent.

❋ Defendant's position

The violation of an OSHA provision can be used as evidence of possible negligence but is not conclusive on its own. The instruction to the jury was improper because, if they concluded the defendant violated OSHA regulations, they had no choice but to find negligence.

❋ Court's response

The Court noted that there was a state statute that provided that nothing in the OSHA regulation shall enlarge, diminish, or affect in any manner laws, duties, or liabilities of employees or employers. If a jury is instructed that an OSHA violation automatically establishes negligence, it reduces the legal burden on the plaintiff. This reduction in the legal burden on the plaintiff in effect changes the laws. The state statute forbids this from occurring.

The Court admitted that other states do consider an OSHA violation to automatically constitute negligence. However, these states do not have a statute controlling the impact of an OSHA violation.

✳ Court's decision
A violation of an OSHA regulation does not make a defendant negligent *per se*. The court set aside the judgment and sent the case back to be reheard by the lower court.

✳ Comments
Even if the OSHA violation is not negligent *per se*, it may influence the jury to the point that a similar result is obtained anyway.

✳ Referenced cases
Brennan v. OSHA 513 F.2d 1032:Federal

Brenan v. Gilles Cotting 504 F.2d 1255:Federal

Otto v. Specialties 386 F.Supp. 1240:Federal

Parker v. South Louisiana Contractors 370 So.2d 1310:Louisiana

National Marine Service v. Gulf Oil 433 F.2d 913:Federal

Clary v. Ocean Drilling 429 F.Supp. 405:Federal

Knoll v. Manatt's Transportation 253 N.W.2d:Iowa

Kelly v. Wright Construction 528 P.2d 500:Washington

Carroll v. Getty UN 498 F.Supp. 409:Federal

Rabar v. duPont 415 A.2d 499:Delaware

Kirkley v. Williams Construction 331 So.2d 651:Alabama

Dunn v. Brimer 537 S.W.2d

Buhler v. Marriott Hotels 390 F.Supp. 999:Louisiana

Case 6

What is the proper measure of damages for negligent construction?

Case name	Kenney v. Medlin Construction & Realty
Decision date	May 15, 1984
Court	North Carolina Court of Appeals
Case cite	315 S.E.2d 311
Plaintiff	Gerry Kenney
Defendant	Medlin Construction and Realty

✳ Prior holding

Judgment of the Superior Court of Cabarrus County in the State of North Carolina was in favor of plaintiff for implied warranty action.

✳ Facts

Medlin Construction and Realty (defendant) signed a contract in 1978 with Kenney (plaintiff) to construct a house for $50,625. Soon after moving in 1979, the plaintiff started to notice signs of distress in the structure. Walls buckled, floors sunk, and the chimney pulled away from the structure—in addition to many other defects. The problems appeared to be caused by differential settlement of the structure.

The jury found that the contractor was liable for the damage and awarded the plaintiff $35,000 (70% of the purchase price). The defendant appealed the decision on several issues, including an improper awarding of damages.

✳ Plaintiff's position

The plaintiff requested that the jury award damages equal to the amount that would be necessary to repair the structure.

✳ Defendant's position

The defendant requested that it would be more appropriate for the jury to provide damages equal to the difference of the price paid and the current value.

✳ Court's response

The court stated that damages are awarded to give the plaintiff an equivalent to what the contract should have provided. There are two methods of measurement for determining damages in construction cases. The first method provides the plaintiff with the amount equal to the cost of repairs (plaintiff's request) and the second method is the difference in value (defendant's request).

The courts noted that typically the cost of repair method of damage measurements is the preferred choice. However, there are circumstances where this method is not practical. It would be against public policy to require a contractor to pay the repair price for a minor deviation in the plans which would result in major costs. If a contractor used material from a foreign country rather than the specification required U.S. material, it would be foolish to make the contractor pay for demolishing the structure when a small monetary damage may be more appropriate. This is assuming that the materials are of equal quality.

The court believed that the defects in this building were of an extent that it was not a minor violation. Utilizing the repair method of calculating damages was appropriate.

✳ Court's decision

The method of calculating damages was appropriate.

✳ Comments

There are situations where damages awarded to a purchaser not only exceed the profit margin of the contractor but may exceed the entire contract amount. This situation can occur when the plaintiff is awarded punitive damages.

Punitive damages are not at all related to the amount of damages suffered by the plaintiff. This type of damage is awarded when it is felt that merely paying back the prevailing party is insufficient to deter the defendant from repeating the unacceptable conduct. A contractor should keep in mind that liability exposure is more than just profits.

✳ Referenced cases

Leggette v. Pittman 150 S.E.2d 420:North Carolina

Robbins v. Trading Post 111 S.E.2d 884:North Carolina

Lagasse v. Gardner 298 S.E.2d 393:North Carolina

Board of Education v. Construction Corp. 306 S.E.2d 537:North Carolina

Coley v. Eudy 276 S.E.2d 462:North Carolina

Blecick v. School District 18 406P.2d 750:Arizona

Jacobs v. Kent 129 N.E. 889:New York

Highway Commissioner v. Helderman 207 S.E.2d 720:North Carolina

Stone v. Homes, Inc. 945 S.E.2d 801:North Carolina

Hartley v. Ballot 209 S.E.2d 776:North Carolina

Case 7

Can implied warranties provided by builder/seller apply to purchasers other than the original purchaser?

Case name	Barnes v. MacBrown and Company
Decision date	February 25, 1976
Court	Supreme Court of Indiana
Case cite	342 N.E.2d 619
Plaintiff	William and June Barnes
Defendant	MacBrown and Company

✳ Prior holding

Court of Appeals in State of Indiana dismissed plaintiff's complaint for breach of an implied warranty.

✳ Facts

MacBrown and Company (defendant) built a house and sold it to Buyer 1. After the house was approximately three years old, it was sold by the original owner to Barnes (plaintiff). After moving into the house, the plaintiff found three large cracks in the basement walls and also that the basement leaked.

The plaintiff sued to recover the costs to repair the walls under a theory of an implied warranty. The lower court dismissed the case on the grounds that subsequent purchasers could not avail themselves of an implied warranty from the builder/seller.

✳ Plaintiff's position

The plaintiff relies on previous court decisions which held that a builder/seller provides an implied warranty to the original purchaser. If this implied warranty is available to the first purchaser, it should also be available to subsequent purchasers.

✳ Defendant's position

The defendant did not directly attack the theory of application of the implied warranty to subsequent purchasers. Their position was that there could only be recovery by the plaintiff for personal injury. An economic loss is not recoverable under these facts.

✳ Court's response

In regards to the plaintiff's argument, the court noted that they had previously abolished the "buyer beware" system of purchasing houses by original buyers from the builder/seller. They admitted that they were well aware that they had to balance the protection of the rights of the contractor with the protection of the consumer. The traditional method of requiring a contractual relationship between the parties is no longer tenable. Implied warranties should be extended to subsequent purchasers if it is reasonable in light of the surrounding circumstances.

The court disposed of the defendant's arguments that the subsequent purchaser could only recover if there was a personal injury. They found no reason under these conditions to distinguish between economic losses and losses from personal injury.

✳ Court's decision

The case was sent back to the lower court to determine, based on the age of the home, its maintenance, and its use, whether or not giving an implied warranty to the subsequent purchaser was appropriate.

✳ Comments

The court made it clear that this case only applied to the situation where defects are hidden. If the defects are discoverable, then the plaintiff is on notice of their existence and can adjust their position accordingly.

It is interesting to note that the court did not give a time limit or a maximum number of subsequent purchasers for the availability of the implied warranty. This is important because a remote purchaser could possibly file suit many years after construction has been completed.

✳ Referenced cases

Theis v. Heuer 270 N.E.2d 764:Indiana

Theis v. Heuer 280 N.E.2d 300:Indiana

Case v. Sandefur 197 N.E.2d 519:Indiana

Campo v. Scofield 95 N.E.2d 802:New York

Uniform Commercial Code 26-1-2-318:Indiana

Case 8

Can implied warranties provided by a builder, who is not a seller, be used by subsequent purchasers?

Case name	Moxley v. Laramie Builders
Decision date	September 27, 1979
Court	Supreme Court of Wyoming
Case cite	600 P2d 733
Plaintiff	Merle and Della Moxley
Defendant	Laramie Builders

✳ Prior holding

District Court of Albany County of the State of Wyoming dismissed plaintiff's complaint for implied warranties for subsequent purchasers.

✳ **Facts**
Laramie Builders (defendant) constructed a home for Owner 1 in 1975. Moxley (plaintiff) bought the home from Owner 1 in 1977. Within two months of purchasing the house, the plaintiff discovered that the electrical wiring in the house was defective and dangerous. Ground fault indicators were not used in areas where water exposure was possible, and some sockets were not properly grounded. The plaintiff filed suit to recover rewiring costs and attorney fees, and also requested punitive damages.

✳ **Plaintiff's position**
The courts have allowed for recovery from the builder under the theory of an implied warranty when the builder is also a seller. The recovery was not limited to the original purchases but was made available to subsequent purchasers as well. There is no legitimate reason why builders who are not sellers should not be held to a similar requirement.

✳ **Defendant's position**
The courts must put a limit on when a builder who is not a seller can be held liable for damages. Allowing the plaintiff to collect under these circumstances would place an overwhelming and unfair amount of liability on the builder.

✳ **Court's response**
The court believed that there should be no difference between a contractor who builds a home on the purchaser's property and a contractor that builds a home on his own property and then sells it to the purchaser. The purchaser expects the same level of quality from the builder as from the builder/seller and both must be equally accountable.

The court was aware of the undesirable position their decision would put the builder in. This decision would leave the contractor in a position of continuing liability long after the home has been built and sold.

✳ **Court's decision**
The court decided that the implied warranties provided by a builder to the original owner are available to subsequent purchasers. The court sent the case back to the lower court for a trial.

❋ Comments

The court, as in the previous cases, stated that the implied warranties were limited to hidden defects. The court also stated that the implied warranties would be available to subsequent purchasers only for a "reasonable length of time." However, no attempt was made to define a reasonable length of time.

❋ Referenced cases

Tavares v. Horstman 542 P.2d 1275:Wyoming

Barnes v. MacBrown 342 N.E.2d 619:Indiana

Coburn v. Lenox Homes 378 A.2d 599:Connecticut

McDonough v. Whalen 313 N.E.2d 435:Massachusetts

Gable v. Silver 258 So.2d 11:Florida

Denna v. Chrysler Corp. 206 N.E.2d 221:Ohio

Nielsen v. Hermansen 166 P.2d 536:Utah

Canon v. Chapman 161 F.Supp. 104:Federal

Cline v. Sawyer 783 P.2d 161:Wyoming

Statute 1-1-109, W.S. 1977:Wyoming

Case 9

Will a release of liability given by the original purchaser be binding for a subsequent purchaser?

Case name	Terlinde v. Neely
Decision date	October 28, 1980
Court	Supreme Court of South Carolina
Case cite	271 S.E.2d 768
Plaintiff	William and Nancy Terlinde
Defendant	J.F. Neely

✳ **Prior holding**

Trial court of the State of South Carolina granted summary judgment to defendant denying implied warranty claim of plaintiff.

✳ **Facts**

Contractor (defendant) built a house in 1972 and sold it to Buyer 1 in 1973. Three years after the purchase, Buyer 1 notified the contractor that there were problems. Contractor agreed to pay Buyer 1 to compensate for the damage and in turn, Buyer 1 signed a release of liability agreement. Later in the same year, Buyer 1 sold the house to Terlinde (plaintiff).

Shortly after the plaintiff purchased the house, additional settlement of the foundation occurred. As a result, brick veneer cracked, doors would not shut properly, and drywall cracked, to name just a few of the problems.

✳ **Plaintiff's position**

The plaintiff's position is the same as that of the previous case (Moxley v. Laramie Builders). That is, the subsequent purchaser should receive implied warranties from the contractor.

✳ **Defendant's position**

Similarly, the defendant has taken the position used in Moxley v. Laramie Builders. That is, the builder should not be liable for an implied warranty for subsequent purchasers. The defendant also had as a defense—the release of liability by the original owner.

✳ **Court's response**

The Court took the position that the builder represents himself as a person with an expertise. The original purchaser as well as subsequent purchasers rely on these representations. A builder owes an implied warranty to subsequent purchasers for hidden defects.

It is interesting to note that the court placed no weight on the fact that the defendant had received a signed release from the original purchaser.

✻ **Court's decision**

The decision of the lower court was reversed and the case was ordered to be heard on the basis that subsequent purchasers receive an implied warranty.

✻ **Comments**

As mentioned, it is interesting as well as disturbing to see that the court ignored the release of liability. From what was reported from this case, it is not known why the liability release was ineffective. The release may have been procured by fraud or was improperly written. Whatever the reason, the lesson to be learned from this case is that a release of liability might not be as powerful as one might tend to believe.

✻ **Referenced cases**

Rutledge v. Dodendoff 175 S.E.2d 792:South Carolina

Lane v. Trenholm 229 S.E.2d 728:South Carolina

JKT v. Hardwick 265 S.E.2d 510:South Carolina

Edwards v. Charleston Sheet Metal 172 S.E.2d 120:South Carolina

Moxley v. Laramie Builders 600 P.2d 733:Wyoming

Brown v. Fowler 279 N.W.2d 907:South Dakota

Barnes v. MacBrown 342 N.E.2d 619:Indiana

Case 10

Can the builder of mass-produced homes be held liable to a purchaser on the basis of strict liability for the failure of a heating system?

Case name	Kriegler v. Eichler Homes, Inc.
Decision date	January 29, 1969
Court	California Court of Appeals
Case cite	74 Cal.Rptr 749
Plaintiff	David Kriegler
Defendant	Eichler Homes

✳ **Prior holding**

Trial court of the State of California allowed plaintiff to recover under the basis of strict liability.

✳ **Facts**

In 1952, Eichler Homes (defendant) constructed a home with an ambient heating system that was buried in the concrete floor slab. Because of the Korean War, there was a copper shortage. Steel tubing was substituted for the copper that would have normally been used for the installation. The substitution had been used in over 4000 radiant heat installations. The steel tubing failed in this house in 1957.

The system allegedly failed because the steel tubing was not uniformly placed in the slab—an act that caused premature deterioration. The magnitude of the failure was such that Kriegler (plaintiff) was forced to temporarily vacate the home and store the furniture.

✳ **Plaintiff's position**

The law allows for the plaintiff to collect damages under a theory of strict liability for the mass production of automobiles. In principle, there is no difference between the mass production of automobiles and of homes. The court should allow for strict liability to extend to mass-produced home construction.

✳ **Defendant's position**

The doctrine of strict liability should not apply to the construction of homes. Strict liability is only appropriate for products. Allowing this theory to extend to home construction would in effect make the contractor an insurer of any problem that could occur in the home.

✳ **Court's response**

The doctrine of strict liability applies when a person is injured, while properly using a product, by a defect in product that the person was unaware of. The court believed that a mass-produced home is no different than a mass-produced product.

When purchasing a mass-produced home, the buyer is relying on the skill of the builder. If an accident occurs as a result of improper construction, public policy dictates that the losses should be carried by the creator of the defect. The contractor is probably in a better economic position to cover the cost of the loss.

✳ Court's decision
Strict liability applies to the builder of mass-produced homes.

✳ Comments
Note the significant advantage to a home purchaser gained by the court allowing them to maintain a strict liability action. Under a strict liability action, the plaintiff need only show a product is defective and not that the defendant is negligent. This significantly reduces the burden on the plaintiff.

✳ Referenced cases
Gherna v. Ford Motor Co. 246 Cal.App.2d 639:California

Vandermark V. Ford Motor Co. 391 P.2d 168:California

Greenman v. Yuba Power 377 P.2d 897:California

Conolley v. Bull 258 Cal.App.2d 183:California

Barth v. Goodrich Tire 265 Cal.App.2d 228:California

Schipper v. Lovitt 207 A.2d 314:New Jersey

Connor v. Great Western Savings 69 Cal.2d 850:California

Vaccarezza v. Sanguinetti 163 P.2d 470 California

Aced v. Hobbs:Sesack Plumbing 360 P.2d 897:California

Case 11

Can a builder be held liable to the purchaser on the basis of strict liability for improperly locating a water heater?

Case name	Hyman v. Gordon
Decision date	December 5, 1973
Court	Appeals Court of California

Case cite	111 Cal.Rptr. 262
Plaintiff	David Hyman
Defendant	Stanley Gordon

✲ Prior holding

Trial court allowed dismissal of case against builder on grounds that the improperly locating of a product does not fall under the theory of strict liability.

✲ Facts

The owner of the home had recently painted and had the paint brushes soaking in a can of gasoline in the garage. Some children had been painting model airplanes in the garage and inadvertently knocked over the can of soaking paint brushes and gasoline. Approximately four feet from where the boys spilled the gasoline was a gas-fired water tank. The gasoline flowed towards the tank and ignited, and the fire caused severe burns to the legs of the plaintiff.

The plaintiff filed suit against the homebuilder (defendant) for strict liability as well as other theories. The court dismissed the strict liability portion of the complaint.

✲ Plaintiff's position

The plaintiff claims that the injuries were caused by the defendant improperly locating the water heater. The selection of where a product should be located should fall under the theory of strict liability. The builder should be liable in tort because the harm resulting from the gas-fired water heater in the garage is foreseeable.

✲ Defendant's position

The water heater was not defective and therefore a strict liability argument is without merit.

✲ Court's response

Strict liability is appropriate for cases that involve defective products. What is a defective product has never been clearly defined. A product may function properly at one location and improperly at others, and therefore location is part of the product responsibility.

✳ Court's decision

The lower court's decision that a strict liability suit was improper for a product location case was incorrect and the case should be reheard.

✳ Comments

This case as in most strict liability cases, tends to represent the position that contractors are better equipped to handle the financial losses from a defect. Although this may be erroneous, it is definitely the trend. This trend may be in line with what the author perceives as the law's continuous turn towards protection of the consumer at the expense of business. The author is not criticizing this trend but rather putting the contractor on notice of its existence.

✳ Referenced cases

Gherna v. Ford Motor Co. 246 Cal.App.2d 639:California

Vandermark V. Ford Motor Co. 391 P.2d 168:California

Greenman v. Yuba Power 377 P.2d 897:California

Conolley v. Bull 258 Cal.App.2d 183:California

Barth v. Goodrich Tire 265 Cal.App.2d 228:California

Schipper v. Lovitt 207 A.2d 314:New Jersey

Connor v. Great Western Savings 69 Cal.2d 850:California

Vaccarezza v. Sanguinetti 163 P.2d 470 California

Aced v. Hobbs:Sesack Plumbing 360 P.2d 897:California

Construction
contracts

There are standard contracts used extensively in construction throughout the United States. These standard contracts are referred to as AIA contracts because they are developed and sold by the American Institute of Architects (AIA). A sample of the contracts available from the AIA includes

➤ A101: Owner-Contractor Agreement for Stipulated Sum

➤ A111: Owner-Contractor Agreement for Cost of Work plus Fee

➤ A191: Owner-Design/Builder Agreement

➤ B141: Agreement Between Owner and Architect

➤ G601: Land Survey Agreement

The AIA charges only a few dollars per blank contract. These contracts are so widely used that it is common for the two parties involved to sign the contracts without having an attorney review it, because both parties are very familiar with the terms and obligations.

The AIA contracts are appropriate for heavy construction, such as the building of bridges and commercial buildings, but they do not lend themselves well to the residential construction industry. In residential construction, the contractor will typically use a contract obtained from other contractors or will have a lawyer draft one. These residential contracts lack the uniformity used in contracts for heavy construction. This is not due to any lack of organization—there are residential contracting associations that provide excellent resources. It is probably more the result of varying local custom that discourages uniformity.

Because a residential contractor is likely to use the same contract over and over, it is foolish not to understand each and every term of the contract. A couple of days spent reading the contract, discussing it with an attorney, and revising it as necessary is time well spent and allows for confidence in the reuse of the contract.

The purpose of the contract is to clearly state the duties and obligations of the parties to avoid litigation. Although every effort is made to provide a contract that meets this standard, it is not always successful.

Some points of the contract that often lead to problems are as follows:

> **Late completion date.** It is difficult for the purchaser to coordinate the time frame of selling an existing home and purchasing a newly constructed home. If the completion date of the new house is not met, it leaves the purchaser without a place to live or a place to store possessions. After a six-month construction period, the purchaser tends to become impatient and sometimes unreasonable. This is further complicated by the fact that the final stages of construction seem to be unproductive to the untrained eye.

> **Warranties.** The purchasers are making the biggest investment of their lives. The costs associated with housing consumes one-third to one-half of the purchaser's income. Needless to say, the purchaser expects near-perfect results. For this reason, the purchaser will often invoke the implied and express warranties to fix the slightest defect.

> **Material substitutions.** Purchasers spend a great deal of time picking and choosing the colors and styles for their house. Substitution by the contractor without prior approval from the purchaser can lead to suspicions on the part of the purchaser that the substituted material is of a lesser quality.

The best-written contract cannot protect the contractor from the ramifications of substandard work and poor judgment. In the event that the parties do disagree, working towards a mutually acceptable agreement is always more productive than letting the lawyers exchange threats. Some suggestions for the contractor to avoid litigation on the construction contract are as follows:

> **Communicate regularly with the purchaser.** Discussions should be had regarding status, changes, delays, and problems. This serves the purpose of letting the purchaser feel involved.

> **Construct with quality.** A structure built in accordance with the specification, drawings, and the proper codes will seldom lead to litigation.

➤ **Plan properly.** Prepare a construction schedule and make a conscious effort to stick to it. Lack of planning leads to delays. Delays lead to unhappy purchasers. Unhappy purchasers lead to litigation.

➤ **Control subcontractors.** The project is only as good as the subcontractors working on it. Check that the subcontractors are doing good quality work in a timely fashion.

This chapter will discuss the various clauses that appear in construction contracts. Appendix A provides a sample contract that utilizes these clauses.

Identify parties

A contract should begin with the identification of the parties that are to be bound by its terms. The information provided should include addresses and telephone numbers of the parties. The business status of all should also be listed (i.e., corporation, sole proprietorship, partnership, etc.).

Descriptions

Both a project and property description should be provided. The project description should briefly describe the style of house to be built, the approximate square footage, and any unique requirements for the project.

The property description should consist of an address location and a legal description. The financier of the project and the contractor will need this information for recording the mortgage and contract, if necessary, with the recorder of deeds. Also, in the event the contractor needs to file a lien against the property due to lack of payment, a time-consuming search through the official records to find the legal description can be avoided.

List of contract documents

The documents that are applicable to the project should be identified. These documents are the design drawings, specifications, local building codes, safety related codes, etc. Identification of the design drawings should include the name of the architect who prepared them.

It is inevitable when multiple codes and specifications are provided that there will be conflicting requirements. This problem can be avoided by noting which documents control in the event of a conflict.

 # Property ownership

For the most part there are two different types of property ownership scenarios. The property may be owned by the contractor who will transfer title when the construction is complete, or the contractor may construct the house on property owned by the purchaser. If the property is owned by the purchaser, the contractor might consider having a title search performed to see if there are any existing liens on the property. Existing liens may possibly subordinate future liens of the contractor. Language should be added to the contract that requires the owner to have all lien encumbrances remedied prior to the start of construction. The contractor should also insist that the purchaser have exclusive and sole ownership of the property. Constructing a building on property that is not fully owned by the contractor or purchaser is risky.

 # Taxes

Taxes and assessments may not come due until the year following their accrual. The taxes and assessments that have accrued on the property prior to its transfer should be prorated to the appropriate party. If the contractor owns the property, it is customary that the contractor pay the taxes and assessments on the property up until the date of transfer of the property to the purchaser.

Purchase price & schedule of payments

The total purchase price of the house should be reflected in the contract. Equally important is the schedule of when payments will be released to the contractor. It is obvious that the contractor should try and obtain as much of the money as early as possible. This will not only help cash flow but also leaves the contractor in a stronger position should the purchaser develop financial problems. It is typical that the contractor be given approximately 10% of the contract amount upon signing, for the purpose of getting mobilized and purchasing insurance and materials. The balance of the contract amount is then paid in three installments, at the following times:

➢ When the roof has been completed

➢ When interior painting begins

➢ Upon completion of the project

Mortgage

The purchaser of the house will most likely need to finance the project with a construction loan, used to pay the contractor at the intervals just described. When the project is complete, the purchaser will then obtain another loan—called an *end loan*—to pay off the construction loan. A construction loan differs from an end loan in that, for the former, interest accrues only on the amount of loan that has been used. For example, if a purchaser were to obtain a construction loan for $200,000, the following might be a breakdown of the payment:

➢ At contract signing (10%) = $20,000

➢ House under roof (30%) = $60,000

➢ Interior ready for painting (30%) = $60,000

➢ Completion (30%) = $60,000

After the house is ready for interior painting, the purchaser will have drawn a total of $140,000 from the loan. Interest would accrue on the $140,000 and not on the entire $200,000.

Once the contract has been signed, the general contractor must be prepared to start work but cannot proceed until the purchaser has obtained the necessary financing. Language should be added to the contract that will obligate the purchaser to make a reasonable effort to get a loan commitment. Otherwise, the contractor may be unable to commit to other work, while the purchaser may not be actively pursuing procuring of the necessary funds. Allowing the purchaser a 30-to-60-day time frame to obtain financing is typical.

A purchaser may try to effectively void the contract indirectly by making little effort to obtain a construction loan. This scenario can be avoided by including a clause that allows the contractor to obtain funding for the purchaser in the event the purchaser cannot. The contract should stipulate that the purchaser is responsible for the fees associated with the mortgage in the event the contractor must assist in procuring the loan.

 # Permits & testing

Permits pose two types of problems. The permit costs money and takes time to obtain. The financial part is typically paid by the purchaser, but the contractor is usually burdened with obtaining them. There are many different permits that are needed for construction projects, and if possible, should be listed in the contract, some of them being these:

> ➤ Building permit

> ➤ Water connection permit

> ➤ Sewer connection permit

> ➤ Site-grading permit

It is not uncommon for the purchaser to provide a set of building plans to the contractor. The contractor will take these plans along with the necessary paperwork and fees to submit to the building department to obtain a building permit. Many times plans provided by the purchaser are incomplete and revisions are necessary. The cost for the necessary revisions of the plans should be paid by the purchaser under these circumstances.

Various tests need to be performed on the building site. These tests include the following:

> **Soil test.** Determines whether the soil has adequate strength to support the loads of the structure. It might also include information on whether the soil types present are susceptible to consolidation, which would produce uneven settlement and result in differential movement of the house.

> **Permeability tests.** If a public sewer system is unavailable, a septic system will be needed. The use of this system is contingent on the soil having enough permeability for the system to function properly. The permeability test will measure how fast water will seep down into the soil.

> **Water quality test.** If a private well system is to be used, a water analysis will be needed to determine if the quality is safe for human consumption.

The contract must clearly state who is responsible for paying for these tests as well as arranging for them.

Time of completion

The purchaser will want the contractor to commit to a date that the project will be completed. A period of six months is usually sufficient to complete the entire project. A clause should be added to extend the deadline if circumstances occur that are beyond the control of the contractor (labor strikes, natural disasters, unavailability of material, etc.).

Some purchasers will include in the contract a fee to be paid for each day the contractor exceeds the completion date. This type of fee is called *liquidated damages*. Liquidated damages are limited to the amount of money the purchaser loses from the contractor's failure to complete the project on time. Unusually large liquidated damage clauses have the appearance of being a penalty rather than a reimbursement cost. Judges will not enforce the liquidated damage clause if it is an excessive amount since assessing penalties is traditionally the function of the court.

The contractor must also obtain assurance that when the structure is complete, the purchaser will not delay in making the final payment and taking possession. It is customary to give the purchaser 14 to 21 days to make arrangements for this transaction.

 # Quality of work

The contract should expressly state that the work of the contractor and all subcontractors shall be in accordance with the drawings and specifications and will meet or exceed certain standards. It shall also be required that all work satisfies the applicable building codes.

 # Materials

Three issues arise when discussing materials:

➤ When does ownership and the subsequent responsibility for the material change from the contractor to the purchaser?

➤ What quality of materials is to be provided?

➤ What about material substitutions?

The material used for the project remains the property of the contractor until the material is installed in the structure. After it has been attached to the structure, it becomes the property of the purchaser. This demarcation identifies ownership for insurance coverage purposes. As an example, assume that the windows for the project are shipped to the site at the end of the day. The windows are to be installed on the next workday. Prior to the start of work the next day, the windows are stolen. The cost of replacing stolen windows would be the responsibility of the contractor. Had the windows been stolen after installation, the replacement liability would be on the purchaser. Obviously the answer to this hypothetical may be different based on local custom or other arrangements.

Under the terms of a contract, the contractor is expected to furnish all material necessary to construct the house. The contract will call for all material to be of good quality, new, and of a quality typically used in the industry.

It is virtually impossible for the contractor to provide a completed house that has been totally in compliance with the owner's color and material requests. Manufacturers discontinue colors and products, and companies go out of business. The contractor must have some flexibility to substitute materials if the specified material is no longer available or not feasible to use. The contract should allow for notification to the purchaser and the purchaser should be allowed a reasonable objection to the substitute.

Change orders

Changes from the original contract, drawing, or specifications have the potential to result in big problems. Additional work is not always welcomed by the contractor because it requires modifying the construction schedule. The purchaser may be skeptical of the costs of the change orders, thinking the contractor may be taking advantage of the situation.

Procedures for the administration of changes in the scope of work must be clearly defined to avoid problems. The following should be addressed in the contract:

> ➤ That a contractor shall not do any work until a valid change order is received.

> ➤ That a change order is not valid unless it is signed by the purchaser.

> ➤ A procedure to handle changes that need to be done immediately.

> ➤ A refusal of contractor to accept a change order.

Insurance

In our previous discussion in this chapter regarding materials, we learned that once the material is installed, it becomes the property of the purchaser. The purchaser must have adequate insurance to cover any losses that may occur during construction. The contractor should request proof of insurance, as well as the right to receive notice if the policy is ever canceled.

Similarly, the purchaser should require that the contractor and subcontractor all carry adequate insurance. Adequate insurance is needed to cover injuries to workers and others on the job site, repairing or replacing damaged property, and workmen's compensation claims. The contractor should have insurance that will pay for the cost of replacing any material that has been damaged or stolen prior to being installed. Because insurance is a complicated subject, you should consult with an insurance broker to determine necessary coverage.

The general contractor should check that all subcontractors are insured. The insurance premiums paid by the contractor are based on the assumption that all subcontractors have insurance. If this is not the case, the contractor's insurance costs will be increased accordingly.

Warranties

Two categories of warranties need to be discussed in regards to the construction contract:

> ➤ Warranties provided by the contractor.

> ➤ Warranties provided by law.

There are two alternatives with respect to warranties provided by the contractor. The first alternative is the typical one-year warranty provided by the contractor. Under the terms of this warranty, the contractor agrees to repair certain defects reported in one year from the completion date. It is important for the completion date to be clearly defined to avoid arguments on when the toll has run on the warranty.

The second alternative is a warranty provided by the contractor that is backed by a third party. As in the previous alternative, the contractor agrees to repair certain defects in the one-year period. If the contractor refuses to make the necessary repairs, the purchaser can make a claim against the third party that backed the warranty.

The other category of warranties is that provided by law (i.e., statute). Some states have enacted legislation that protects the purchasers of new homes. These laws require that the general contractor provide a certain level of quality as well as a limited warranty. Examples of warranties provided by law are as follows:

> ➤ **Implied warrant of merchantability.** This warranty provided in the Uniform Commercial Code states that a seller of goods must provide goods that meet the minimum level of quality established in the industry.

> ➤ **Implied warranty of fitness for a particular purpose.** This warranty, also provided by the Uniform Commercial Code, states that if the general contractor knows the purpose the structure is being used for, and if the purchaser is relying on the skills of the general contractor to select and furnish suitable goods, then there is an implied warranty that the general contractor shall provide goods for that purpose.

> ➤ **Implied warranty of habitability.** Several decades ago, the legal system would employ the Doctrine of Caveat Emptor— better known as "buyer beware." This line of thinking basically takes the position that when the purchaser buys the house, all defects were now the problem of the purchaser. Caveat Emptor is no longer followed; the courts' position is now that the general contractor provides an implied warranty that the house is in a habitable condition.

In the absence of a written warranty, these three implied warranties can be utilized by the purchaser. Construction contracts often include clauses that explicitly exclude these warranties as well as any other implied warranties. These disclaimers will significantly reduce the liability of the contractor and limit the remedies available to the purchaser.

Safety

Safety is one of the most important issues in construction. A general contractor has a moral obligation to ensure the safety of the worker as well as a financial interest to avoid unnecessary costs and time loss. Because the purchaser is not regularly on the job site, it usually is the general contractor's responsibility to provide a safe working environment. Unfortunately, this responsibility brings a considerable amount of liability with it. The general contractor should work diligently to have a safe work site.

Subcontractors

The general contractor is responsible for ensuring that all work performed by subcontractors is performed in an acceptable manner and in accordance with the contract, design drawings, and specifications. The general contractor shall not use any subcontractors who are not fully insured as required by this contract or any subcontractor reasonably objected to by the purchaser. The contractor shall not be required to hire any specific subcontractor unless expressly specified in the contract. In addition, each subcontractor should be required to acquire liability insurance and workmen's compensation insurance for all of their on-site employees.

Destruction of premises

The structure may be destroyed by any of a variety of natural disasters, as well as by vandalism. When such unfortunate events occur, there must be no ambiguities as to the available options to the parties. One way to handle this situation is to permit the contractor the choice of one of the following options:

Chapter 6

➤ Take the insurance proceeds and rebuild the structure.

➤ Void the contract, receive the insurance proceeds, and return any deposit money received.

The contract should allow the contractor two weeks to decide on one of the two options.

Utilities

The general contractor shall be responsible for arranging for permanent utility connections, as well as for the cost incurred to provide utility service to the residence. All costs incurred for utility services prior to the closing shall be paid for by the general contractor. The general contractor shall notify all utility companies prior to any digging to avoid damage to buried service lines.

Clean up

The general contractor shall keep the construction site in a neat and clean condition during the life of this contract, regardless if the work is being performed by the general contractor or a subcontractor. All material shall be stored in an orderly, neat, and safe manner. The entire premises—interior and exterior—shall be cleaned immediately prior to closing, including removal of all trash and debris.

Punch list

As the project nears completion, the contractor usually has some odds and ends that need to be finished to be in full compliance with the contract. This minor work should not prevent the transfer of title and the corresponding possession to the purchaser. After the structure has been substantially completed, a punch list is prepared and the purchaser takes over ownership. A punch list specifically lists the work needed to achieve final completion of the contract. It is the contractor's responsibility to complete the items on the punch list within a reasonable time—typically thirty days.

Assignment of contract

A valid contract provides each of the parties with a certain amount of limited rights, one of them being the option of selling the benefits and obligations of the contract to another party. The transfer of benefits and obligations is called an *assignment of the contract*. Assignment of a contract is typically discouraged in construction because a change in either the contractor or purchaser can lead to a multitude of problems. It would be prudent to forbid either party from assigning the contract.

Default

The contract must address the possibility that one of the parties may end up defaulting on the contract. A procedure should be clearly presented in the contract to handle this situation to minimize the damage.

Default is determined as follows:

> **Contractor default.** Purchaser shall make a written demand questioning the lack of progress. If the contractor fails to respond in 10 days, the purchaser can consider contractor in default.

> **Purchaser default.** If purchaser fails to make a required payment, the contractor shall make a written protest of the missed payment. If the purchaser does not make payment in 10 days, the contractor can consider the purchaser in default.

Arbitration

A thorough discussion of arbitration is presented in Chapter 11. A typical clause inserted into a contract to provide for arbitration is

> Any controversy or claim arising out of or relating to this
> contract, or the breach thereof, shall be settled by arbitration in
> accordance with the Construction Industry Arbitration Rules of
> the American Arbitration Association and judgment upon the
> award rendered by the arbitrator or arbitrators may be entered in
> any court having jurisdiction thereof.

The insertion of this clause into the contract provides for arbitration
should a dispute arise. Alternate methods of arbitration or dispute
resolution are available in addition to the American Arbitration
Association referenced in the clause. Arbitration has many benefits
over a court trial; for example, it's expeditious, economical, and
informal.

However, arbitration does have drawbacks. First, the arbitrator is the
judge of what evidence can be heard and is not required to follow the
federal and state rules of evidence. In a court trial, the parties can
predict fairly well what can be admitted as evidence, but this is not
the case in arbitration. Another drawback is that there is little chance
of the court overturning a bad decision by the arbitrator.

Although there are some problems with arbitration, it is nevertheless
a very efficient manner of dispute resolution in the construction
industry. The parties should consult an attorney, and the applicable
rules on arbitration, to determine if this is the method desired to
settle disputes.

Specifications

Documents that must be complied with in regards to a particular construction project are provided in the construction agreement. The following contract clause is typical of what would be found in a residential construction contract:

> The following items are hereby included as part of the contract:
>
> - Design drawings
> - Specifications
> - Local building codes
> - Any applicable portion of the Occupational Safety and Health Code (OSHA)
> - Local fire codes
> - All applicable material codes
>
> In the event these documents are in conflict, the order of precedence shall be as listed here.

If the contractor failed to follow the documents listed here, he would be in breach of contract. Therefore, it is always important to review the contract to be on notice what the building requirements are.

Design drawings are the most important part of the construction documents, as evidenced by their lead position in the list. Design drawings provide the necessary dimensions, member sizes, and other essential information. But even the most detailed drawings cannot list all the information needed to construct a house, which is why design drawings must be supplemented with specifications. *Specifications* are written instructions that provide detailed information on products, material, and performance requirements.

Specifications are technical in nature—they are not prepared with a legal state of mind, but rather in the interest of satisfying architectural and engineering requirements. But, due to their importance, the specifications often become the center of litigation. A quality set of specifications, followed closely by the contractor, will steer the parties clear of lawsuits.

Because the specifications become part of the contract by reference, their importance cannot be overstated. This chapter will provide an overview of what information is detailed in the specifications.

Excavation

Excavation work can lead to a multitude of problems. Unexpected buried boulders, improperly located utility lines, and very wet soils can cause delays and may even totally frustrate the project. The specifications should list the work to be performed by the contractor, as well as the work that is not covered under the contract. A possible breakdown of the costs may be as follows:

Contractor costs

➤ Remove tree or brush growth

➤ Strip and stockpile soil

➤ Foundation excavation

➤ Foundation backfilling

➤ Spreading topsoil after project completion

Purchaser costs

➤ Additional grading of site beyond spreading of topsoil

➤ Removal and disposal of any buried items

 # Foundation concrete

The strength of the concrete that is required shall be specified. Because the strength of the concrete changes as it cures, a standard measurement at a specific time must be used. The measurement standard that is used in the industry is the strength when the concrete is 28 days old. The amount of steel reinforcing and the size of the individual bars to be used in the foundation should be provided in the specifications.

Steel members

It is common to use circular steel pipe columns to support the first floor. If circular steel pipe columns are to be used, the minimum allowable diameter should be specified and whether the columns will be hollow or filled with concrete. The size of the steel beams should also be provided.

Steel comes in many different levels of quality. A reference standard should be listed for the purpose of obtaining a steel of a quality that is suitable for residential construction.

Foundation wall covering

The exterior side of the foundation wall that is to be covered with dirt should be coated with an asphalt-based or similar material. This coating will prevent or reduce water infiltration through the concrete wall. Water infiltration may result in premature deterioration of the wall, as well as allow moisture to get into the basement. These coatings can be sprayed or brushed onto the wall. Any weather restriction conditions that may adversely affect the products should be enumerated.

Note that there is a distinct difference between waterproofing and dampproofing. *Waterproofing* prohibits moisture penetration, while *dampproofing* does not prohibit but rather inhibits the moisture migration. Accordingly, dampproofing is less expensive than waterproofing.

Footing drain

The location of the natural ground water level can be from a foot to many feet below ground level, depending on the topology of the land. This natural water causes a significant increase in the lateral pressure on the foundation wall and can also result in uplift of the basement slab. These pressures can be reduced by the use of a foundation drain system.

A foundation drain system is constructed of a perforated continuous plastic pipe around the circumference of the foundation next to the footing. The water in the soil near the wall drains into the gravel that is placed around the pipe and then into the holes in the pipe. Once the water is in the pipes, it flows into the sump pit in the house and is pumped up and out of the basement to a location away from the foundation.

The specifications should provide information on the material and size of the piping as well as the material it will be placed in. It should also require that the material meet ASTM standards.

Walls, floors, ceilings, & truss framing

Information that should be provided in this section includes

Walls

➤ Size of studs

➤ Spacing of studs

➤ Type of wood

Floors & ceilings

➤ Range of member sizes

➤ Type of wood

➤ Bracing requirements

Trusses (site-built)

➤ Member sizes

➤ Type of wood

➤ Bracing requirements

Trusses (prefabricated)

➤ Designed to carry loads

➤ Drawings to be stamped by a licensed engineer

Roofing

The specifications regarding the roofing should include information on warranties and material. The warranty should be divided into labor (usually one year) and material (usually in excess of 10 years).

The material needed for the roofing is shingles and felt paper. Roofing shingles are specified by their weight. The greater the weight of the shingle, the longer the life expectancy.

Exterior items

➤ **Windows.** Because the quality of windows varies greatly, it is important to distinguish the particular make and model that will be provided.

➤ **Gutters & downspouts.** The material and sizes should be listed.

➤ **Garage doors.** The specifications should note whether the garage doors will be wood or steel. If wood is chosen, then the type of wood and the finish (paint or stain) shall be provided in the specifications. In colder climates, it should be noted whether the steel doors will be insulated.

Sewer system

The wastewater from the house must be either disposed of on site with a septic system or sent for treatment to a wastewater plant. If the latter is used, a connection to the public sewer system will be required. This work includes excavation, furnishing and installing the connection piping to the trunk line of the public sewer. The septic system installation includes providing and placement of the stone, filter paper, pipe lines, septic tank, and excavation.

 # Concrete slabs

Information that is needed in regards to the concrete slab is:

➤ **Minimum thickness of stone base.** An adequately compacted stone base is necessary to provide good drainage characteristics and to prevent differential settlement that could cause the concrete to crack.

➤ **Reinforcement.** In most cases, a welded wire fabric is used in the concrete slab to reduce unsightly cracking.

Depending on local soil conditions, a layer of visqueen may be placed in the stone to prevent the migration of moisture from the soil up through the slab.

 # Plumbing

Most people associate plumbing with water supply and wastewater removal. The plumbing work also includes installing the sinks, hot water heater, and sump pump.

Certain work items cannot be adequately estimated prior to construction. For example, it is difficult to estimate how deep a well will need to be until the drilling has started. For this type of item, the general contractor gives the purchaser an allowance, where the allowance is an estimate of the price for the work. After the work has been completed, the price is adjusted upward or downward accordingly. The following list is what would be provided as per the plumbing specifications:

Water

➤ Piping for all sinks, bathrooms, dishwasher, water heaters, and all other items that require water

➢ 50-gallon hot water heater

➢ Well

➢ Kitchen sink

➢ Utility sink

➢ Shower bases

➢ Faucets

➢ Exterior faucet

➢ Sump pumps

➢ Water softener

Wastewater

➢ Piping from all sinks, bathrooms, etc.

➢ Septic system

Gas

➢ Gas piping from exterior source to furnaces, stoves, fireplace log lighter, dryer, and water heater.

Allowances

➢ Septic $X,XXX

➢ Water softener $X,XXX

➢ Well $X,XXX

➢ Plumbing fixtures $X,XXX

Heating & insulation

The specifications should clarify the number of furnaces to be provided as well as the make and model.

The amount and efficiency of the insulation affects not only the heating and cooling costs, but also the comfort level for the inhabitants. The *R* number, which is the measure of the efficiency of the insulation, should be clearly stated in the specifications to avoid substandard insulation being installed.

Interior items

➤ **Paint.** List number of coats. Also specify if colors other than white will result in an extra charge.

➤ **Wood trim & doors.** List what type of material will be used for trim and doors. List whether doors and trim will be painted or stained.

➤ **Finished floors.** The following is a sample of what information is provided in the specifications in regards to this item:

Ceramic tile shall be installed at the following locations:
• Foyer
• Kitchen
• Dinette
• Bathrooms

The allowance for ceramic tile is $X,XXX.

Carpet shall be installed at the following locations:
• Bedrooms
• Family room
• Office
• Living room
• Dining room
• Stairs
• Upstairs hallway

The allowance for carpet is $X,XXX.

All flooring is placed on ¾-inch tongue and groove, with ¼-inch underlayment and 4 × 8 sheets of plywood. Plywood is glued to joists.

Summary

Drawings cannot provide all the necessary information required to construct a house, so specifications must be prepared.

Specifications are written instructions that provide detailed information on products, material, and performance requirements.

Specifications are important and can often become the center of litigation.

Because specifications become part of the contract, their importance cannot be overstated.

A list that provides the relevant items to be included in the specifications is provided in the "Forms" sections of this publication.

A sample specification is also provided in Appendix B.

Subcontractor
contracts

General contractors are paid by the owner for their expertise in construction management. One of the most important tasks of a construction manager is the coordination of the subcontractors. Some smaller homebuilders will also perform construction services in their field of expertise; however, most large homebuilders rarely perform any construction services and subcontract each and every item of construction project.

All of the subcontractors will directly contract with the general contractor. On large construction projects, these contracts can be in excess of a hundred pages. In contrast, subcontracts for residential construction are typically one page or may even be based on oral agreements.

A typical one-page residential subcontract/general contractor agreement typically contains the following:

➢ Start date

➢ Expected completion date

➢ Price

➢ Payment terms

➢ Outline of work

It is questionable whether the use of such a sparse contract is wise. Possible reasons for why these agreements have traditionally contained so little detail include the following:

➢ Subcontractors often work with the same general contractors; therefore, the parties see no need to have a detailed legal arrangement.

➢ General contractors usually are too busy to take the time to work on a detailed agreement.

➢ Subcontractors may not be willing to sign a long detailed contract.

➢ It is the standard of the industry and people are reluctant to change.

Whatever the reason, it might be prudent for the general contractor to consider requiring the subcontractor to sign a detailed contract. If a valued subcontractor is reluctant to sign a detailed contract prepared by the general contractor, the general contractor has to weigh the benefits of the protection of the detailed contract to the ramifications of losing a good subcontractor.

The remainder of this chapter will be devoted to presenting topics that would be properly addressed in a detailed contract between a subcontractor and a general contractor.

Parties to the contract

As in any contract, the name of the parties and their form of ownership should be listed in the contract.

Description of work

A detailed description of the work to be performed by the subcontractor is a necessary component of the contract. It is recommended that the subcontractor provide a list of the work to be performed, because it will be more thorough than if the general contractor prepared it. The description of the work can be provided as an appendix to allow for the body of the contract to remain unchanged for the sake of uniformity.

Applicable documents

The subcontractor must perform the work in a manner consistent with what is expected of the general contractor. This is best handled by listing in the subcontractor/general contractor agreement the documents that are binding on the general contractor in the owner/general contractor agreement. These documents can include the following:

➢ drawings

➢ specifications

➢ building code

➢ fire code

➢ OSHA

Permits

It is usually more expeditious for the party performing the work to arrange for any necessary permits. The parties should agree as to who will pay the associated permit fees, although it probably is already known from industry custom.

Document examination

A statement should be included that provides that the subcontractor has reviewed the plans, specifications, and other pertinent documents. It should also include a statement to the effect that the subcontractor has made a site visit prior to agreeing to the terms of the contract. This contract language will prevent the subcontractor from trying to obtain extra costs, based on a claim of lack of knowledge of conditions.

Financial terms

The financial terms that need to be addressed in the contract go beyond just the listing of the agreed-upon price. Other items that need to be addressed are the time of payments, billing procedures, and retainage.

Some subcontractors have low cash flow due to the small size of their operations. It might not be in the general contractor's best interest to pay the subcontractor immediately upon completion of the work. Payment within 30 days after completion of the work is a reasonable time period for the subcontractor to receive payment and allows the general contractor time to review the work for conformance with the contract. This time period may also allow the contractor to obtain another payout from the owner.

The subcontractor should be instructed in the agreement what is the proper billing procedures. The proper procedure should require that the subcontractor provide a waiver of lien for the applicable work and for any materials used. The payment procedure should identify the person to send the invoice to, as well as any other requirements of the contractor.

It is possible that problems may develop with respect to the subcontractor's portion of the work. A problem that often occurs is that the subcontractor has not finished every detail of the work. It might be difficult for the general contractor to get the subcontractor back to the project site if the subcontractor has already been paid in full. The general contractor may withhold a certain percentage (usually 10%) until a few months after the subcontractor's work is completed. This sum of money, called *retainage*, provides the incentive for the subcontractor to complete any unfinished or any defective work.

Warranties & instructions

The general contractor will provide warranties to the owner typically for a period of one year, although the general contractor is most likely not doing any of the actual work. The general contractor should get the subcontractors to provide the same warranty as the general contractor provides to the owner; this would prevent the general contractor from having to fix warranty related problems caused by a subcontractor that is no longer legally required to fix the problem.

Mechanical equipment such as furnaces, air conditioning, dishwashers, etc., are covered by warranties provided by the manufacturer. The owner of the house will need to fill out the necessary paperwork and send it to the manufacturer to obtain the warranty. The owner will expect to receive the necessary paperwork as well as the equipment manual from the general contractor. The general contractor must make this material available to the owner, but the subcontractor who installs the equipment will be in possession of the information. The general contractor should include a term in the contract that requires the subcontractor to provide this information in a timely fashion to avoid having to spend time trying to track it down later.

Time of completion

The general contractor is bound to a completion date in the general contractor/owner agreement. The general contractor has the ultimate responsibility for a missed completion date. The subcontractor that caused the delay might have completed the work and been paid months ago. For the general contractor's protection, the general contractor/subcontractor agreement should list the maximum amount of days the subcontractor will have to complete the work. The time when the toll begins to run should be clearly presented in the contract to prevent disagreements as to the subcontractor completion date.

Disruptions in the construction schedule beyond the control of the subcontractor might occur. The contract must address what occurrences will qualify for extensions in the contract completion date.

Default

Due to the risky nature of construction, it's not inconceivable that a general contractor or a subcontractor might default on the contract. Accordingly, the parties must address what will be considered a default and what remedies are available to the nondefaulting party.

A default for a subcontractor can be defined as failure to perform substantial work within 10 days of notice. A default for a general contractor can be defined as failure to pay within so many days of completion or failure to provide a start date within so many days of signing of the contract.

The remedy for the general contractor for the default of a subcontractor should be the cost to complete the work that exceeded the contract cost. The remedy should also include the costs of attorneys and court fees necessary to obtain reimbursement resulting from the default. The remedy for the subcontractor from the default of the general contractor should be the lost profits on the remainder of the contract, plus any attorney or court fees expended to obtain payment or reimbursement.

Safety

The general requirements of safety are presented in Chapter 9, which notes (among other things) that safety, to some degree, is everyone's responsibility. The general contractor/subcontractor agreement, in certain terms, should define what is expected of each of the subcontractors. Chapter 9 also notes that the project requires that information in emergency facilities be provided, first aid equipment be available, workers be provided with proper protection equipment, etc. The general contractor and subcontractors should review what safety measures and equipment are needed and who will provide and maintain this equipment. Safety is a serious issue, and the parties need to address it not only at the time of contract formation but also during construction.

The Occupation Safety and Health Act has requirements for the recording of injuries. The responsibility of the subcontractor to fully comply with these and similar requirements should be noted in the agreement. It is in the best interest of all parties that they be notified immediately of any injuries. The general contractor or owner may need to take immediate action to avoid a similar accident or may suggest more substantial treatment for an injury. This cannot be done if the owner and general contractor are not notified of the accident in a timely fashion.

The subcontractors bring their own equipment to the job site. Because the subcontractors might have other projects, this equipment is often moved up and back between construction sites. This constant movement makes it difficult for the general contractor to inspect each and every piece of equipment. The general contractor would be prudent to add a contract clause that notifies the subcontractors to inspect and maintain their own equipment so that it is always in a safe condition.

Indemnification

If the subcontractor is negligent or commits any of the variety of torts, it is inevitable that the injured party will sue the general contractor—which is typical, regardless of how remotely responsible (if at all) the general contractor is for the injury. The general contractor can avoid being liable for the torts of the subcontractor by adding an indemnification clause to the contract. This clause should contain language that provides for the subcontractor to pay any damages awarded against the general contractor for a tort committed by the subcontractor.

Insurances

The cost of insurance to the general contractor is estimated on the assumption that all the subcontractors will purchase insurance. At the end of the year, the project, or at some other designated time, the insurance provider will require that the general contractor provide a list of all the subcontractors that were used. The insurance provider will require that the general contractor provide proof of insurance for each of the subcontractors. The general contractor should provide contract language that not only requires the subcontractors to obtain insurance but also requires that proof of this insurance be provided before any work is started. Note that the requirements that the subcontractor be fully insured is often a clause in the general contractor/owner agreement.

Contract with owner

It is recommended that only the general contractor have direct communication with the owner to avoid conflicting instructions as well as outright confusion. Contract language should be added that requires any and all correspondence be sent directly to the general contractor. This contract clause should also specifically state that the subcontractor shall do work at the direction of the general contractor. This statement will prevent the general contractor from getting stuck in the middle of a situation where the subcontractor believes extra work has been done and the owner thinks the work is part of the contract.

The owner may decide to expand the scope of the construction project. For example, the owner halfway through the project might decide that it would be desirable to have a concrete driveway. The general contractor would get an estimate from a concrete subcontractor, add profit and overhead costs, and submit a proposal to the owner. The general contractor would like to avoid the situation where the subcontractor goes directly to the owner with the proposal. Not only would this situation result in a loss of profits, it will also cause potential coordination problems. The general contractor should have language that forbids any subcontractor from directly contracting with the owner during the duration of the project.

 # Available utilities

Some of the subcontractors will need utilities, especially electricity, to perform their services. The subcontractor's bid might be based on the assumption that electricity, or other utilities, will be made available by the general contractor. If electricity is not available, the subcontractor will have to make arrangements to have this service provided by using gas-fueled generators. The general contractor should clarify if electrical service, or any other required utility, will not be provided. Although the cost associated with providing these temporary services is not significant, the impact of lost workdays associated with this problem might be costly.

 # Quality of work

The general contractor will be bound by the general contractor/owner agreement to provide a structure that meets some level of quality. Phrases often included in the agreement are "of workman-like quality" or "of a quality consistent with local custom." Because the general contractor is required to build a quality structure, it would be wise to obligate the subcontractor to provide work of at least the quality needed to satisfy the owner. This can be handled by using the same language in the subcontractor agreement that is used in the general contractor/owner agreement.

Clean construction site

The general contractor is interested in a clean construction site for three reasons. First, the owner is expecting to receive a quality-built new structure. If the subcontractors do not totally clean up from their work, it will become the responsibility of the general contractor. The associated costs are a direct drain on profits. Second, a messy construction site is a violation of safety rules because it increases the possibility of injury. Third, the general contractor's reputation is at stake on every project, and a messy construction site does not enhance one's reputation.

The contract with the subcontractor should address what is expected of the subcontractor in regards to cleanup. Both final and continuous clean-up obligations should be stated.

Material substitution

The owner has a right to a reasonable rejection of substitutions of materials. The general contractor should list this right in the subcontractor agreement to be able to enforce the reasonable objection right of the owner in regards to the subcontractor.

Assignment of contract

The general contractor should be sure to specify in the contract that the subcontractor cannot assign the contract. If the subcontractor were allowed to assign the contract to another party, the general contractor might end up dealing with an undesirable and unexpected third party.

 # Summary

Contracts between general contractors and subcontractors for most construction projects are detailed and can be as much as several hundred pages.

Contracts between general contractors and subcontractors for residential construction have traditionally been lacking in specifics and only one or two pages long.

It is questionable if such short contracts are useful to avoid problems in determining legal obligations.

The contract between the general contractor and the subcontractor should contain a detailed description of the work to be performed by the subcontractor.

The documents that are binding on the subcontractor should be specifically listed.

It should be noted what party is responsible for obtaining and paying for permits.

The subcontractor should specifically state that by signing the contract, the subcontractor has read all of the applicable documents and has visited the construction site.

The subcontractor should address how and when payment will be made to the subcontractor.

Warranties to be provided or not provided shall be clearly noted in the subcontract.

The subcontractor should commit to a date on which construction will be completed. However, provisions should be made for an extension of time for circumstances beyond the control of the subcontractor.

Default on the contract is always a possibility in construction and the parties must have a mechanism in place that will definitely determine when a party is in default, as well as the remedies available to the nonbreaching party.

Safety, to some degree, is everyone's responsibility. What is expected from each party in regards to safety should be noted. The subcontractor should notify the general contractor immediately of any accidents on the project.

The subcontract should require that the subcontractor fully comply with Occupational Safety and Health rules, including the use of equipment that is safe and properly maintained.

The subcontractor should indemnify and hold harmless the general contractor for any torts committed by the subcontractor.

The cost of insurance for the general contractor is based on the use of properly insured subcontractors. The subcontract should set the amount of insurance required to be carried by the subcontractor.

The general contractor may find it desirable to prevent the subcontractor from contracting directly with the owner.

If utilities are not going to be available to the subcontractors, the subcontract should reflect it.

The subcontract should state that the subcontractor shall perform all work in a workman-like manner and of good quality.

The general contractor shall require that the subcontractors keep the construction site clean. This will reduce any clean-up costs for the general contractor, reduce the possibility of accidents, and enhance the contractor's reputation.

The subcontract should not be assignable to any party.

9

Safety

Without question, the most important part of any construction project is the safety of any and all persons at the work site. Keeping a work site in a safe condition is not only a moral obligation but has serious financial ramifications. Failing to maintain an accident-free work area invites financial disaster for everyone involved.

The following information provided by the Bureau of Labor Statistics provides some very interesting insight into injuries in the construction industry:

➢ In a given year, approximately 14 out of every 100 construction workers are injured. This is the worst record of any of the major industries.

➢ In a given year, approximately 1 out of every 10 residential construction workers is injured.

➢ Half of all injured construction workers will have lost workdays as a result of their injuries.

➢ Residential construction has the lowest accident incidence rate of any of the types of construction.

According to the National Safety Council, injuries cost an average of nearly $1000 per worker per year, while the average fatality approaches one million dollars in associated costs. There are many more statistics to further emphasize the fact that injuries cost money; however, just these facts are compelling enough.

The construction industry obviously needs a safe working environment; what we need to decide is who is *responsible* for providing this safe working environment. In my opinion, everyone has a responsibility for creating and maintaining a safe construction site, but these participants all have varying degrees of responsibility based on their control of the work.

You should note that, even though each of the parties has varying degrees of responsibility, an injured party will typically file suit against anybody remotely connected to the project. Because of this mentality, it is in the best interest of every entity involved to have a completely safe project from start to finish.

In the early 1970s, the Federal government enacted the Occupational Safety and Health act (OSH). The purpose of the OSH act was to force all employers to provide a safe workplace for employees. The OSH act also created the Occupational Safety and Health Administration (OSHA) to enforce the OSH rules. OSHA has the power to enforce the OSH rules and levy substantial fines to any employer that is not in compliance with safety rules.

The OSH rules are a product of Federal law. Individual states are entitled to enact their own rules in regards to employee safety. However, the rules enacted by an individual state must be at least as strict as those provided by OSH.

The OSH rules are located in the Federal Register, which provides the text of the Federal laws. The Federal Register is divided into 50 topics (called *titles*). OSHA Safety Rules and Health Standards are located in Title 29: Labor. In particular, Part 1926 of Title 29 pertains specifically to the construction industry and is divided into the following 24 subparts:

A General
B General Interpretations
C General Safety and Health Provision
D Occupational Health and Environmental Controls
E Personal Protective and Life Saving Equipment
F Fire Protection and Prevention
G Signs, Signals, and Barricades
H Material Handling, Storage, Use, and Disposal
I Tools
J Welding and Cutting
K Electrical
L Ladders and Scaffolding
M Fall Protection
N Cranes, Derricks, Hoists, Elevators, and Conveyors
O Motor Vehicles, Mechanized Equipment and Marine Operation
P Excavations, Trenching, and Shoring
Q Concrete, Concrete Forms, and Shoring
R Steel Erection
S Tunnels, Shafts, Caissons, Cofferdams, and Compressed Air
T Demolition

U Blasting and Use of Explosives
V Power Transmission and Distribution
W Rollover Protective Structures, Overhead Protection
X Stairways and Ladders

A brief viewing of this list may give the impression that most of the topics are unrelated to residential construction. Actual review of the document itself reveals a significant amount of requirements that must be followed by the homebuilder.

The remainder of this chapter will be devoted to discussing generally what is of interest in each of these subparts. This discussion, due to space limitations, is not a comprehensive list of requirements. Any person interested in a complete understanding of the applicable requirements should consult the entire document.

A: General

This subpart sets forth the general safety and health standards from the Secretary of Labor. From a technical viewpoint, there is nothing of interest in this subpart.

B: General Interpretation

This subpart contains the general rules of the Secretary of Labor regarding applying the OSHA provisions. Of interest in this subpart is what OSHA calls the rules of construction. A summary of these rules are:

> 1926.16(a): The prime contractor and the subcontractor may make their own arrangements as to who will take care of the obligations of the rules. But in no case shall any arrangement relieve them of the legal responsibility for compliance.

> 1926.16(c): The prime contractor assumes the entire responsibility under the contract for complying with the rules. With respect to subcontracted work, the prime contractor and subcontractor shall be deemed to have joint responsibility.

C: General Safety and Health Provisions

This subpart provides definitions and general rules for the Act. A summary of these rules are:

1926.20: Employers are not to have employees work in unsafe environments and shall provide and maintain programs as necessary to comply with the Act.

1926.21: The employer shall instruct each employee in the recognition and avoidance of unsafe conditions.

1926.23: First aid services and provisions for medical care shall be made available by the employer for every employee covered by the regulations.

1926.25: Debris shall be kept clear from work areas, passageways, and stairs. Containers shall be provided to collect waste.

1926.28: Note that protective equipment must be provided in accordance with Subpart E.

D: Occupational Health and Environmental Controls

Items discussed in this subpart usually do not pertain to new residential construction. Items in Subpart D include regulations for asbestos removal, respirator requirements, and noise exposure. There are two items of considerable interest as given in the following:

1926.50(a): Provisions shall be made prior to the commencement of the project for prompt medical attention in case of a serious injury.

1926.50(f): Telephone numbers of the physicians, hospitals, or ambulances shall be conspicuously posted.

E: Personal Protective and Life Saving Equipment

The items of importance are:

1926.100: Employees working in areas where there is a danger of head injury from impact, or from falling or flying objects, shall be protected with protection helmets.

1926.102: Employees shall be provided with eye and face protection equipment when machines or operations present potential eye or face injury.

F: Fire Protection and Prevention

Discussion of this section is omitted because it is assumed that there is an adequate supply of water and fire fighting equipment nearby, the electrical work will be in accordance with code, and all combustible material will be properly stored.

G: Signs, Signals, and Barricades

This section would rarely ever apply to residential construction.

H: Materials, Handling, Storage Use, and Disposal

The majority of this subpart discusses the lifting of materials. Safe lifting of materials requires proper lifting devices as well as their proper connection to the material to be lifted. Other items of interest in this subpart are:

1926.250(a)(1): All material shall be safely stacked.

1926.252(a): Whenever materials are dropped more than 20 feet to any point lying outside the exterior wall, an enclosed chute shall be used.

1926.252(b): Whenever debris is dropped through a hole in the floor without the use of a chute, the area onto which the debris is falling should be enclosed with barricades.

1926.252(c): All scrap lumbers, waste material, and rubbish shall be removed from the immediate work area as the work progresses.

I: Tools

According to OSHA 1926.300, all hand and power tools and similar equipment shall be maintained in a safe condition. This requirement applies not only to tools furnished by the contractor but those furnished by the subcontractor or any employee. The following are some of the regulations in regards to tools that are used in the residential construction industry:

1926.300(b): When power tools are designed to accommodate guards, they shall be equipped with such guards when in use.

1926.300(d)(3): Certain hand tools such as circular saws, chain saws, and specific types of percussion tools shall be equipped with a constant pressure switch that will shut off the power when the pressure is released.

1926.301(d): The wooden handles of tools shall be kept free of splints or cracks and shall be kept attached to the tool.

1926.302(a)(2): The use of electric cords for hoisting and lowering tools shall not be permitted.

1926.302(a)(4): All pneumatically driven impact tools that operate at more than 100 psi pressure shall have a safety-switch device on the muzzle to prevent tools from ejecting fasteners unless the muzzle is in contact with the work surface.

J: Welding and Cutting

This subpart rarely applies to the residential construction industry. Note that cutting in the subpart title refers to torch cutting, not saw cutting.

 # K: Electrical

This subpart presents the requirements for providing a safe working environment with respect to electricity. The subpart is divided into four sections.

> Installation Safety Requirements: 1926.402 through 1926.408. These sections are quite comprehensive with respect to electrical equipment and installation used to provide electric power and light on the job site. It is recommended that the reader review this entire section in the OSHA regulations if it is applicable.

> Safety Related Work Practices: Some of the more pertinent requirements of this section include:

> > 1926.416(a)2: In work areas where the exact location of underground electric power lines is unknown, employees using jack-hammers or other hand tools which may contact a line should be provided with insulated protective gloves.

> > 1926.416(e)(1): Worn or frayed electrical cords or cables shall not be used.

> > 1926.416(e)(2): Extension cords shall not be fastened with staples, hung from nails, or suspended by wire.

> Safety Related Maintenance and Environmental Considerations: Probably the only requirement that is on point is 1926.432(b), which provides that the material used should be appropriate for the environment it will be exposed to.

> Safety Requirements for Special Equipment: This section is not applicable to typical residential construction.

L: Scaffolding

Although scaffolds are extensively used in construction, they have a more limited use in residential construction. Scaffold use is limited to attachment of the exterior facade and for drywalling high ceilings and painting. OSHA addresses over 20 different types of scaffolding from motorized to swinging. Tubular frame scaffold is probably the most common type used and the reader is referred to sections 1926.451(c) and (d) to review specific requirements for this system.

General requirements for all scaffolding is located in Section 1926.451(a). The requirements of interest in residential construction are as follows:

1926.451(a)(2): The footing or anchorage for scaffolds shall be sound, rigid, and capable of carrying the maximum intended load without settling or displacement. Scaffold or planks shall not be supported on anything unstable.

1926.451(a)(3): A competent person shall supervise construction and dismantling of the scaffolding.

1926.451(a)(4): If the platform is higher than 10 feet above ground or the floor, guardrails and toe boards shall be provided. Scaffolds between 4 and 10 feet high that are 4 feet long or wide shall have guardrails.

1926.451(a)(7): Scaffolds and their components shall be capable of supporting four times the maximum intended load.

1926.451(a)(8): Damaged or weakened components of the scaffold system shall be removed or replaced or repaired.

1926.451(a)(10): All planking shall be scaffold grade or equivalent. The maximum permissible spans for various working loads are shown in Table 2-3 of OSHA.

1926.451(a)(12): All planking of platforms shall be overlapped a minimum of 12 inches or secured from movement.

1926.451(a)(14): Scaffold planks shall extend over their end supports not less than 6 inches or more than 12 inches.

1926.451(a)(17): Slippery conditions on scaffolds should be taken care of as soon as possible.

M: Fall Protection

This subpart applies to temporary or emergency conditions where there is a danger of employees or materials falling through floor, roof, or wall openings. The most significant regulation in this subpart is 1926.500(c)(8) which requires that floor holes into which people may walk shall be guarded by a railing or covered up. A floor opening is any opening measuring 12 inches or more in the least dimension through which a person may fall.

N: Cranes, Derricks, Hoists, Elevators, and Conveyors

The machinery discussed in Subpart N is not often used on residential construction sites.

This subpart goes through great lengths to make it clear that if the machinery is not specifically for lifting or transporting employees, it shall not be used for such.

O: Motor Vehicles, Mechanized Equipment and Marine Operations

This section deals with various items for construction equipment including:

1926.600(a)(3)(i): When parked, set parking brakes and, if on an incline, chock wheels.

1926.600(a)(5): All cab glass shall have no distortion and shall be safety glass.

1926.601(a)(2)(ii): All vehicles shall have brake lights.

1926.601(a)(5): All vehicles with cabs shall have windshields with powered wipers.

1926.601(a)(9): Seat belts shall be installed in all motor vehicles.

1926.604(a)(2): All equipment used in site clearing operations shall be equipped with rollover guards.

P: Excavations, Trenching, and Shoring

Excavating can lead to many dangerous conditions in construction. Appropriately this subpart has one of the more detailed regulations of OSHA. Before getting into specific regulations, it is worthwhile to look at a brief overview of this subpart. Subpart P is divided into the following sections:

1926.650: Definitions
1926.651: General Requirements
1926.652: Requirements for Protective Systems
1926.652(a): Protection of Employees
1926.652(b): Design of sloping and benching systems
1926.652(c): Design of support systems
1926.652(d): Materials
1926.652(e): Installation of supports
1926.652(f): Sloping and benching systems
Appendix A: Soil Classifications
Appendix B: Sloping and Benching
Appendix C: Timber Shoring
Appendix D: Aluminum Shoring

Appendix E: Alternatives to Timber Shoring
Appendix F: Selection of Protective System

In the ensuing discussion, the following is assumed:

➤ You're familiar enough with excavating such that the definitions of 1926.650 are known.

➤ The use of a shoring system is not efficient from a cost standpoint.

➤ The excavation is not less than five feet. This assumption is made because an excavation less than five feet coupled with an examination by a competent person that there is no indication of a cave-in does not require any protective measures.

➤ The excavation will not exceed 20 feet.

➤ Any excavation is open for 24 hours and therefore no short term benefits are permitted.

➤ Soil is uniform throughout the depth of the excavation.

Using these assumptions, the only sections of interest in Subpart P are:

1926.652(b): Design of Sloping and Benching Systems
1926.652(f) Sloping and Benching Systems
Appendix A: Soil Classifications
Appendix B: Sloping and Benching

The *Design of Sloping and Benching Systems* of 1926.652(b) provides four options for an excavation that will not utilize shoring:

❶ Use a side slope of two feet vertical to every three feet horizontal (34°).

❷ Use Appendix A and B of Subpart P to find an appropriate side wall slope.

❸ Design slope using other available published data.

❹ Have a registered professional engineer approve any slope design.

Option 1 is a straightforward method of determining the side slope of an excavation. This option requires no information gathering or analytical procedures. Option 2 requires some analytical work but has a trade-off in that it may allow for a more liberal slope, and therefore a cost savings, over Option 1. Option 3 and 4 will not be considered here, as the former is not usually practical and the latter is not cost-effective.

As noted, Option 2 requires more analytical work than Option 1. With Option 2, the soil is first classified. Based on the type of soil an appropriate slope is chosen. The three possible soil classifications are

Type A: Soils that are predominately clay.
Type B: Soils that are predominately silty.
Type C: Granular soils such as gravel and sand.

Type A soil is the most cohesive and allows for a steeper sloped excavation. Type C soil is of a nature that is less cohesive and more likely to cave in.

The maximum slopes for each of these soil types are

Type A: Three horizontal, four vertical (53°).
Type B: Three horizontal, three vertical (45°).
Type C: Three horizontal, two vertical (34°).

Remember that if the contractor does not desire to do any soil classification, Option 1 allows the choosing of a 34° angle slope. Comparison to the maximum slopes for the three soil types reveals that Option 1 is actually the choosing of the worst soil type.

If the contractor can or does not want to use a sloping system, then the details of Subpart P with respect to shoring should be reviewed.

Q: Concrete, Concrete Forms, and Shoring

The items of interest are:

1926.701(a): No construction loads shall be placed on a concrete structure or portion of a concrete structure unless the employer determines, based on information received from a person who is qualified in structural design, that the structure or portion of the structure is capable of supporting the loads.

1926.703(a): Formwork shall be designed, fabricated, erected, supported, braced, and maintained so that it will be capable of supporting without failure all vertical and lateral loads that may reasonably be anticipated to be applied to the formwork.

1926.703(d): Employers shall take measures to prevent unrolled mesh from recoiling. Such measures may include, but are not limited to, securing each end of the roll or turning over the roll.

R: Steel Erection

This subpart applies to structures that have steel framing that is more sophisticated than that typically used in residential construction.

S: Underground Construction, Caisson, Cofferdams, and Compressed Air

It would be extremely rare that any of these regulations would apply to residential construction.

T: Demolition

This book is limited to new residential construction and demolition regulations are not applicable. If the reader is interested in demolition requirements, than this subpart should be consulted because the regulations are quite extensive.

U: Blasting and the Use of Explosives

This subpart would not be applicable for residential construction.

V: Power Transmission and Distribution

This subpart is not applicable to residential construction.

W: Rollover Protective Structures, Overhead Protection

This subpart is not applicable to residential construction.

X: Stairways and Ladders

This subpart deals with stairways, fixed ladders, self-supporting portable ladders, and portable ladders that are not self-supporting. Stairways and fixed ladder regulations will not be covered because portable ladders are much more common to the residential industry. Some of the pertinent regulations of this subpart are as follows:

1926.1053(a)(1)(i & ii): Each ladder shall be designed to carry at least four times the maximum intended load.

1926.1053(a)(2): Ladder rungs, steps and cleats shall be parallel, level, and uniformly spaced when the ladder is in position for use.

1926.1053(a)(3)(i): Rungs, steps and cleats shall be spaced not less than 10 inches apart nor more than 14 inches apart, as measured along the ladder's side rails.

1926.1053(a)(4)(ii): The minimum clear distance between side rails for all portable ladders shall be 11.5 inches.

1926.1053(a)(6)(ii): The rungs and steps of portable metal ladders shall be corrugated, knurled, dimpled, coated with skid resistance material, or otherwise treated to minimize slipping.

1926.1053(a)(7): Ladders shall not be tied or fastened together to provide longer sections unless they are specifically designed for such use.

1926.1053(b)(1): When portable ladders are used for access to an upper landing surface, the ladder side rails shall extend at least three feet above the upper landing surface to which the ladder is used to gain access.

1926.1053(b)(2): Ladders shall be maintained free of oil, grease, and other slipping hazards.

1926.1053(b)(3): Ladders shall not be loaded beyond the maximum intended load for which they were designed.

1926.1053(b)(4): Ladders shall be used only for the purpose for which they were designed.

1926.1053(b)(5)(i & ii): Non-self-supporting ladders shall be used at an angle such that the horizontal distance from the top of the ladder to the foot of the ladder is approximately one-quarter of the working length of the ladder. For wood job-made ladders with spliced side rails, this should be reduced from one-quarter to one-eighth.

1926.1053(b)(6): Ladders shall be used only on stable and level surfaces unless secured to prevent accidental displacement.

1926.1053(b)(7): Ladders shall not be used on slippery surfaces unless secured or provided with slip-resistant feet to prevent accidental displacement.

1926.1053(b)(8): Ladders placed in any location where they can be displaced shall be secured to prevent accidental displacement or barricades.

1926.1053(b)(9): The area around the top and bottom of ladders shall be kept clear.

1926.1053(b)(11): Ladders shall not be moved, shifted, or extended while occupied.

1926.1053(b)(15): Ladders shall be inspected by a competent person for visible defects on a periodic basis and after any occurrence that could affect their safe use.

Summary

The most important part of any construction project is safety.

Failure to keep an accident-free work area invites financial disaster for everyone involved.

In a given year, approximately one out of every 10 residential construction workers is injured.

In the early 1970s, the Federal government enacted the Occupational Safety and Health act (OSH) for the purpose of forcing employers to provide a safe workplace for employees.

The OSH act created the Occupational Safety and Health Administration to enforce the OSH rules.

The OSHA regulations are divided into 24 subparts.

Subpart B, General Interpretation: Regardless of the agreement between the general contractor and the subcontractor, the former is not relieved of safety responsibilities.

Subpart C, General Safety and Health Provisions: Working environments shall be kept safe, first aid and medical attention shall be made available, debris shall be collected, and protective equipment shall be provided.

Subpart E, Personal Protective and Life Saving Equipment: If needed, employees shall be provided with head and eye protection.

Subpart H, Material Handling, Storage Use, and Disposal: Materials shall be lifted in a safe manner, safely stacked, not dropped more than 20 feet if not in a chute, and shall be cleaned up as soon as possible.

Subpart I, Tools: All tools shall be maintained in a safe condition, equipped with guards and a constant pressure switch if applicable, and have a safety switch device if it is an impact device in excess of 100 psi pressure.

Subpart K, Electrical: The regulations with respect to electrical hazards are quite extensive. This subpart is divided into the four sections of Installation, Work Practices, Maintenance and Environmental Considerations, and Special Equipment.

Subpart L, Scaffolding: The regulations provide requirements for a multitude of scaffolding; however, most of these are not used in residential construction. General requirements include proper anchorage, competent supervision for erection and dismantling, guardrail for platforms higher than 10 feet, loading requirements, and planking details.

Subpart M, Fall Protection: Floor holes must be covered or have guardrails.

Subpart O, Motor Vehicles: Motor vehicles shall be safely parked, have properly operating brake lights, seat belts, and rollover guards if applicable.

Subpart P, Excavation: Excavation should be shored or have sloped sides to prevent cave-ins. Sloped sides are the most common method of cave-in prevention. The angle of the slope is dependent on the type of soil.

Subpart Q, Concrete: No loads shall be placed on concrete unless it is capable of carrying the loads.

Subpart X, Ladders: The regulations for ladders are extensive. Regulations include loading, dimensions, and many other important safety considerations.

10

Mechanic's liens

Contractors are in an unfortunate position when the owner refuses to pay for work performed. Material and services provided by the contractor cannot necessarily be repossessed as those in other industries. This problem is further compounded by the industry custom of paying contractors after performance.

A contractor cannot survive for very long if owners are not prompt with payment. The contractor must maximize cash flow while minimizing payment problems. Use the following suggestions to reduce the occurrences of payment problems:

> ➢ Procure a significant portion of payment for the project prior to starting work.

> ➢ Investigate the financial resources of your client.

> ➢ Require the client to place money designated for the project in an escrow account.

> ➢ If it is feasible, stop work when payment is not being received on a regular basis.

Regardless of the measures taken, there will still be occasions when payment will not be received. As previously discussed, the contractor has limited options because repossession is impractical if not impossible. Fortunately, each state's legislature recognized the unenviable position of the contractor and so enacted mechanic's lien laws.

The mechanic's lien laws are a set of rules that help the contractor receive payment for labor, material, and services—accomplished by allowing the contractor to "lien the property" of the owner for an amount equal to the enhancement from the construction. Without the use of a mechanic's lien, legal action could unfold as follows:

❶ Contractor completes work or an agreed portion of the work.

❷ Owner refuses to pay for work.

❸ Contractor files breach of contract action against owner.

❹ Owner sells property.

❺ Contractor wins breach of contract action.

❻ Old owner files for bankruptcy.

❼ Contractor receives portion of bankruptcy funds or possibly nothing.

With the availability of mechanic's lien laws, the scenario can now unfold as follows:

❶ Contractor completes work or an agreed portion of the work.

❷ Owner refuses to pay for work.

❸ Contractor files mechanic's lien action.

❹ Owner sells property. However, new owner will take property subject to mechanic's lien.

❺ Contractor wins mechanic's lien action.

❻ Old owner files for bankruptcy.

❼ Owner receives money due from the present or past owner or can force the sale of the property to satisfy the debt.

If there is no previous judicial opinion on a particular issue in a state court, the judge of that state will very often allow the attorneys to argue their case with the support of judicial opinions from other states. This is based on the theory that the opinions given by judges in other states have some value in deciding issues never before addressed. An exception to this rule is when mechanic's liens are involved. Each state has different variations of mechanic's lien laws, which means that judges of any state will give no credence to mechanic's lien case decisions rendered by judges from other states. For this reason, it is highly recommended that the contractor obtain the mechanic's lien laws of the appropriate state because the laws of other states will be inapplicable. You should keep in mind that the rules presented in this chapter might differ from those used in your state.

The logistics of a mechanic's lien action are fairly straightforward. If the contractor does not receive payment, the contractor files a *notice of mechanic's lien* with the office of the recorder of deeds. This document puts the entire public on notice that the contractor is owed money for work on the subject property. Within a certain time frame, the contractor must initiate suit to enforce the lien.

Obviously, the mechanic's lien laws provide the contractor with a powerful tool for obtaining payment for services rendered and materials provided. Because of this extra advantage given to the contractor, judges will strictly construe the law against the contractor. In other words, all time limits, restrictions, and rules of the mechanic's lien act must be followed exactly. The intelligent contractor should have a copy of the mechanic's lien law and have a thorough understanding of the applicable portions; if a significant amount of money is at stake, the services of an attorney are almost mandatory.

A mechanic's lien action does not preclude the contractor from filing a breach of contract action. Mechanic's liens are just an additional method for obtaining payment. Most likely, if the contractor loses a mechanic's lien action, the filing of a breach of contract would not be allowed at a later date. The rules will typically require that all issues be settled at the same time the mechanic's lien action is being heard.

Mechanic's lien laws protect a wide variety of contractors and subcontractors. The following is a partial list of those typically covered by the mechanic's lien act:

➤ Concrete contractors

➤ Formwork suppliers

➤ Excavators

➤ Architects

➤ Structural engineers

➤ Land surveyors

➤ Well drilling contractors

➤ Material suppliers

➤ Remodeling contractors

➤ Landscape contractors

➤ Wood-framing contractors

➤ Laborers

Mechanic's lien laws differ for general contractors and subcontractors. It is important to be cognizant of the difference in the rules because classification as a subcontractor typically mandates a stricter set of provisions.

A general contractor is defined as a party that contracts directly with the owner or owner's representative of the owner. A subcontractor is an entity that has a contract directly with the general contractor. Most statutes classify material suppliers as subcontractors.

With regards to the general contractor, a sample of some of the requirements are as follows:

➤ Before receiving payment, it is the duty of the general contractor to provide the names and addresses of all parties furnishing materials and labor. This list must include the amount due these parties and must be signed under oath. The purpose of this requirement is to provide the owner with notice of the subcontractors and suppliers who have performed work on the property.

➤ General contractors must file notice of a lien with the recorder of deeds or file suit for not receiving payment within four months after completion of the project to receive full protection under the mechanic's lien laws. If notice of the lien is filed after the four-month period, the contractor loses priority lien status and will be in line behind any party that has filed a previous lien. This rule serves an important purpose in that it forces the general contractor to file a lien within four months if priority status is desired. Therefore, any party lending money to the owner with the property being used as collateral or any other general contractor doing work need only be concerned about services performed by others in the previous four months.

➤ The general contractor must file suit within two years of completion of the contract.

➤ There must be a valid contract between the owner and the general contractor.

With regards to subcontractors, a sample of some of the requirements are as follows:

> ➤ There must be both a valid contract between the subcontractor and the general contractor as well as between the owner and the general contractor.

> ➤ For residential construction, the subcontractor shall notify the owner within 60 days of starting, that labor and material are being furnished. If notice is given after 60 days, the lien amount is reduced by the amount the owner has been prejudiced by payments made prior to notice being received.

> ➤ The subcontractor must file a lien with the recorder of deeds within four months of job completion to maintain priority and then file suit within two years. These are the same requirements for a general contractor.

Comparison of the requirements for the general and subcontractor shows that there are additional requirements for the latter. The reason for this disparity is that there tends to be unknown subcontractors on just about every project. The timing requirement makes the owner aware of the subcontractors' existence providing the owner with notice that these subcontractors need to be paid.

Mechanic lien laws will also provide information on what party has preferential liens. The preferential lien is important not only because it will determine who will get paid first, but it is important if the owner goes bankrupt. In a bankruptcy proceeding, there is more money owned to creditors than is available for payment. Based on the order of preference of payment, some parties will get full payment and others will get partial payment or nothing at all. The order of preferences typically is as follows:

❶ Claims for wages

❷ Claims of subcontractors in proportion to amount due

❸ General contractor receives balance

From this discussion, you should see that there are advantages and disadvantages to having subcontractor status. The advantage is that the subcontractor can get preferential status over the general contractor. However, the subcontractor has to comply with stricter rules that must be followed in order to satisfy the mechanic's lien act.

The existence of a mechanic's lien act poses some logistic problems. Property owners often will not pay the general contractor without proof that the subcontractors and material suppliers have been paid. The general contractor might not have the cash flow to pay the subcontractors while awaiting payment from the owners. This stalemate is usually settled by the subcontractors providing the general contractor with proof of payment (called a *lien waiver*), even though payment has not been received. This places the subcontractor in a precarious position by giving up one's lien rights while trusting the general contractor to make payment. However, if the general contractor takes advantage of the subcontractor in this situation, it could result in criminal charges in some states.

The availability of the mechanic's lien act are not a guaranteed right for the contractor. Owners are aware of the detrimental effects liens can have on a parcel of property. For this reason, owners have often added a clause that takes away the lien rights of the contractor. A sample of this type of contract clause (often called a non-lien clause) is

> The contractor agrees to provide a completed project that is free from all liens and encumbrances.

This clause will extinguish the rights of the contractor to file a mechanic's lien against the property. Some states have laws that forbid the owner from using such a clause. Other states have taken the position that the owner has a constitutional right to contract freely with respect to the property.

The real controversy with respect to no-lien clauses is when it controls the subcontractor's mechanic's lien rights. Many courts have held that when the owner and contractor agree to a no-lien contract, the subcontractor may not file a mechanic's lien. This is disturbing in the sense that the subcontractor is held to the terms of the contract to which the subcontractor is not a direct party to. In fact, in many instances, the subcontractor is not even aware of this no-lien clause agreement between the owner and general contractor.

Courts are divided into two groups in relation to the issue of the subcontractor's rights under a no-lien contract between the owner and general contractor. The first category takes the position that the subcontractor's rights are derivative of the general contractor and that, if the general contractor does not have the right to enforce a lien action, the subcontractor also cannot. The position is harsh on the subcontractor.

The other category of judicial decisions is the position that the subcontractor's rights to a mechanic's lien are direct and therefore the general contractor cannot bargain these rights away.

A middle of the road position on this issue is that the general contractor-owner agreement can extinguish the mechanic's lien rights of the subcontractor only if notice is given that the contract forbids liens. The following are the possible methods that may be considered proper notice in various states:

> ➤ Sign posted on project that project will be lien free.

> ➤ Recording of the contract in the office of the Recorder of Property Deeds.

> ➤ Written notice by certified mail to the subcontractor.

> ➤ A signed writing by the subcontractor agreeing to the no-lien contract.

A no-lien clause provides no benefit to the subcontractor or general contractor, so it is in the best interest of the general contractor to have the clause deleted if possible from the construction contract. If the owner will not allow the clause to be deleted, the general contractor shall be careful to be certain that there are sufficient funds to finance the project.

The subcontractors should always inquire whether the project is under a no-lien contract. A review of the owner-general contractor agreement would normally state if the contract is no-lien. The subcontractor might need to inquire further because a no-lien clause may be contained in a separate agreement. It may also be advisable for the general contractor to notify the subcontractor of the no-lien clause. Although there might not be an affirmative duty to notify, being up front with the subcontractor may reduce the general contractor's liability as well as avoid future litigation.

Residential construction is typically done within the private sector and most often will not have any government involvement. It is unlikely but still possible that some residential construction projects might be government funded. Mechanic's lien action will typically have different requirements when public funding is involved. If a general contractor gets involved in a residential construction project with government funding, it would be wise to confer with counsel or read the appropriate statutes to avoid inadvertently forfeiting the benefits bestowed by the mechanic's lien laws.

Remember that the mechanic's lien rules are different for *every* state—which means that the contractor *must* become familiar with the law of the state where the construction project is located.

 # Summary

States have passed laws which allow a contractor to place a lien against property when work was performed but payment was not received. This type of lien is called a mechanic's lien.

Mechanic's lien laws differ from state to state.

Mechanic's lien laws provide a set of guidelines that must be followed for the general contractor to have a valid lien.

In particular, the mechanic's lien laws provide deadlines for when a lien must be filed with the recorder of deeds and the last day a suit may be brought to enforce the mechanic's lien.

The courts will most likely strictly enforce the requirements of the mechanic's lien act so it is imperative that the contractor follow them closely.

Subcontractors can also utilize the benefits of the mechanic's lien laws. Subcontractors are broadly defined in the statutes to involve a wide variety of construction-functions from excavators to landscapers.

The requirements are usually more restrictive for subcontractors than for general contractors.

There may be additional mechanic's lien law requirements for contractors in residential construction than in other types of construction.

Owners can add clauses to construction contracts that prevent the filing of a mechanic's lien action. These are called *no-lien* clauses. No-lien clauses effectively extinguish the lien rights of the general contractor and possibly even the subcontractor. Contractors would be wise to avoid a contract with this type of clause.

Arbitration

If you are employed in the construction industry, you know that problems in a construction project are inevitable. There are unforeseen delays, discrepancies in the drawings, and unanticipated site conditions—just to name a few. The vast majority of these problems are typically not of a significance that costs or scheduling will be affected and are handled cordially between the owner and contractor. Because of the complexity of construction, situations will arise where parties will not be able to come to an agreement.

Litigation costs are a direct drain on both the profits of the contractor and the investment of the owner. Regardless of which party prevails in the courtroom, there seldom is a clear winner in construction litigation because the winner will rarely receive all damages, attorney fees, court costs, and lost work-time. Owners and contractors are prudent if they reach a mutually acceptable agreement when problems occur.

If an amicable agreement cannot be reached by direct negotiation, the parties typically turn to litigation. Parties retain lawyers, file claims, counterclaims, interrogatories, and take depositions. But there *is* an alternative to these rigors of litigation: arbitration.

Arbitration is an arrangement whereby the disputing parties agree to tell their side of the story to another disinterested party. Prior to beginning the arbitration procedure, both parties agree to abide by the decision of the disinterested party. After hearing all sides of the story, the disinterested party (called the *arbitrator*) will decide who is right and who is wrong.

Parties are free to agree to whatever arbitration agreement is best for their situation. They can have disputes settled by mutual friends, use the arbitration services of a nonprofit organization, or utilize the services of a for-profit arbitration company.

Regardless of how the parties plan to have the arbitration proceeding administered, there must be an agreement on what the rules will be. Parties must agree on what evidence the arbitrator will hear, if the decision must be by a majority or a unanimous decision, where hearings will be held, etc. For arbitration to function properly, the parties must be in agreement on all of these details. It is obvious that a contract to achieve all of this would need to be quite extensive.

Parties often agree to follow arbitration rules composed by companies that provide arbitration services or by nonprofit organizations that exist for the purpose of fostering arbitration, which avoids forcing the parties to write their own detailed arbitration agreement. One of the most popular collection of arbitration rules is provided by the not-for-profit American Arbitration Association, whose function is to administer arbitration between parties who have agreed to do so. To reach this end, the AAA has put together a set of arbitration rules called "Construction Industry Arbitration Rules," which provide over fifty different guidelines to be followed by parties desiring to utilize the arbitration process. Because these rules are used extensively in the construction industry, we'll spend the rest of this chapter examining some of their more important points.

Parties can agree to use arbitration before problems arise or can agree to arbitration after the problem develops. If the parties agree to arbitrate at a time prior to a problem arising, the following clause in their construction contract would be sufficient to send matters to arbitration:

> Any and all controversies arising out of this contract shall be settled in accordance with the Construction Industry Arbitration Rules of the American Arbitration Association. Any judgment rendered by the arbitrator shall be binding and upheld in any court having proper jurisdiction.

If the parties agree to arbitrate after a problem has occurred, the following agreement would provide for arbitration.

> The parties listed at the end of this document have agreed to settle a dispute as outlined in the remainder of this agreement. Arbitration shall be in accordance with the "Construction Industry Arbitration Rules" of the American Arbitration Association. The decision of the arbitration shall be binding on the parties listed below and upheld by the court having proper jurisdiction.

These contract clauses to make arbitration binding are fairly straightforward and easily understood, and both reference the "Construction Industry Arbitration Rules" of the American Arbitration Association. For arbitration to be effective, the applicable rules must be thorough while keeping the arbitration process fair and expedient. Before a party agrees to arbitration, it would be wise to review and have a basic understanding of the rules that will be applied. A complete listing of the "Construction Industry Arbitration Rules" by the American Arbitration Association is given in Appendix C. Several of the more important issues with regard to these rules will be discussed in the remainder of this chapter.

The main ingredient to a successful arbitration is a qualified arbitrator. First and foremost, this person must be neutral and disinterested in the outcome. Any prior relationship with the parties or interest in the outcome of the case must be disclosed and dealt with appropriately.

Under the Construction Industry Arbitration Rules, each party is provided with an identical list of qualified arbitrators, compiled from a pool of arbitrators whose qualifications are acceptable to the American Arbitration Association. The parties review the list of potential arbitrators and eliminate the names of those that are found to be objectionable. The remaining names of acceptable arbitrators are then sent to the American Arbitration Association. They will review the shortened lists and will submit arbitrators that should be acceptable to both sides. If the parties do not agree to use any of these appointed arbitrators, the American Arbitration Association will choose the appropriate party to be the arbitrator. Note that if this process of choosing an arbitrator is unacceptable, a clause can be added to the construction contract that can override the discussed method.

The arbitration clause in the contract can also provide the number of arbitrators that will decide the case. Increasing the number of arbitrators may result in increased costs if the arbitrators are paid for their services, but having two or more arbitrators can be beneficial because two heads are better than one. Unless otherwise specified, the Construction Industry Arbitration Rules assume there will be one arbitrator.

The rules require only a majority decision from the arbitrators. Parties that desire a unanimous decision to decide the case should state this in their arbitration agreement. The reasoning behind the arbitration decision is not required to be disclosed or detailed because the courts feel such a disclosure would probably lead to more litigation. The award decision itself must be in writing and signed by the majority.

The arbitrating parties are allowed to use attorneys and, in situations where significant sums are at stake, would be advised to have adequate representation. The case's complexity will also determine the desirability of the use of legal counsel. In any case, the opposing party should be notified of the intended use of an attorney.

Although the American Arbitration Association and other similar entities are not-for-profit, there is a fee associated with the arbitration hearing. These fees are used to cover the costs of administrative fees of the American Arbitration Association and are based on a percentage of the amount being sought by the parties.

When the amount in controversy does not exceed $50,000, an expedient procedure is available. This expedited procedure follows the regular arbitration rule but adds a few modifications:

➢ Arbitrators are chosen in a different manner. Under the expedited rules, each party is given a list containing the names of five arbitrators. Each party may strike two names from the list. The arbitrator is then chosen from the unstricken names.

➢ The arbitrator's decision shall be rendered within 14 days as opposed to the usual 30-day period.

➢ All notification can be done by telephone.

Arbitration has advantages over traditional litigation, being less costly and more quickly resolved. However, agreeing to arbitration without considering some potential problems can lead to some disastrous results. The following text will present problems that can occur when arbitration is chosen to settle disputes. If these items are of concern to you, consult an attorney to determine the appropriate language to add to the contract in order to avoid those potential problems.

The Construction Industry Arbitration Rules provide that "The arbitrator may grant any remedy or relief that the arbitrator deems just and equitable within the scope of the agreement of the parties . . ." This clause raises several concerns. For the most part, judges are elected officials or are chosen by elected officials, and this elective process provides some stability that the court's decision will be reasonable. An arbitrator has no relation to an elected office, which removes some measure of checks and balances from the system. In fact, the arbitrator need only answer to the American Arbitration Association because courts are very unlikely to change an arbitrator's decision. A second consideration is that arbitrators can award punitive damages, usually for the purpose of punishing a party or sending a message that the behavior of the losing party is not acceptable. It is questionable if such power should be given to an arbitrator.

Rule 11 of the Construction Industry Arbitration Rules states that the parties may mutually agree on a locale where the arbitration will be held. If the parties cannot agree, the American Arbitration Association shall determine the locale and that decision shall be final and binding. This rule might result in a party arbitrating at a location that is inconvenient and unexpected. Obviously such a result would reduce the benefit of the convenience offered by arbitration.

Rule 31 of the Construction Industry Arbitration Rules states that the arbitrator shall be the sole judge of what evidence will be considered. The rule further states that the legal rules of evidence need not be applied. The legal rules of evidence are a complex and thorough set of rules that were developed by legislators, judges, and attorneys over a considerable length of time, and are supposed to be fair, practical, and meet constitutional requirements. Furthermore, those litigating under these rules can have reasonable expectations of what evidence will be heard, as well as the impact of the evidence on their case. With arbitration, these elements of fairness and reliance on what evidence will be admissible are no longer guaranteed because the arbitrator need not follow these rules and can make the sole decision of what evidence will be heard.

Arbitration clauses should be reviewed carefully to ensure that they are not one-sided clauses. A one-sided arbitration clause provides only one of the parties with the option to utilize arbitration. This puts the party with the arbitration option in a superior position in that they alone decide the forum for dispute resolution. Their choice of forum may inconvenience the other party and will obviously be chosen to provide the best odds of winning.

Expectations of the arbitration clause applicability is that it covers only construction-related issues, but without any limiting language in the arbitration clause, this is most likely not the case. For example, an owner might want to hire a contractor that has experience in a particular type of project (for example, hazardous waste removal). Based on the general contractor's representation, the owner agrees to sign a contract. If the owner later finds that the general contractor fraudulently misrepresented qualifications and experience, the owner might desire to have the contract voided based on the theory of fraud. However, the owner may be precluded from bringing an action in the courts because arbitration was the agreed method of dispute resolution. The scope of the arbitration is no longer construction issues but has instead become a complex legal issue. It would be prudent to limit what issues will be covered by arbitration when the clause is drafted. Remember, both parties are free to agree to any arbitration rules they desire—as long as they both agree to them.

Arbitration has proved to be a successful and expedient way of solving disputes, but it also has its problems. The contractor should resolve potential problems prior to agreeing to this forum.

 # Summary

Arbitration offers an alternative to litigation whereby parties have agreed to settle their disputes by letting a disinterested party decide liability.

Parties have unlimited options in regards to arbitration. They can mutually agree on the choosing of any party as the arbitrator or can make use of for-profit or not-for-profit organizations that assist in the administration of arbitration.

The first step is to agree to arbitrate. The second step is to agree to what rules will be applicable to the arbitration. The second step is crucial since the rules of arbitration can have either little or extensive detail. The extent of the detail of the rules has a relationship to the successfulness of the arbitration.

The Construction Industry Arbitration Rules of the American Arbitration Association are a commonly used set of rules to settle construction disputes.

The arbitration rules must provide for the selection of a qualified and neutral arbitrator. Also, the number of arbitrators to hear the case should be specified.

The parties to the arbitration can make use of legal counsel, but the opposition should be notified.

When agreeing to arbitration, the agreement should clearly address the following:

> Location of hearings

> Type of damages the arbitrator can award

> What rules of evidence shall apply

> What issues can be settled by arbitration

12

Pretrial litigation

Due to the complexity of construction coupled with the public's propensity to sue, it is not uncommon for a construction company to find themselves in the position of defending a lawsuit. In some situations, it might be serious enough that the outcome of the lawsuit will determine if the company will remain in existence.

The contractor must take an active role in any lawsuit filed against the company. Involvement will not only assist in achieving a more favorable disposition of the case, but it will help the contractor to keep a handle on the legal costs. The contractor should give proper respect to the judgment of the legal counsel but should not be intimidated by the complexity of the legal arena. This chapter (and the following one) will provide the contractor with a working knowledge of the legal system, as to allow for intelligent and informed participation.

Well over ninety percent of lawsuits that are filed never make it to an actual trial. The majority of cases are settled or dismissed *after* being filed but *prior* to the start of a trial. This time frame is called *pretrial*. This chapter will concentrate on pretrial issues, and the next will look at what occurs if the case does proceed to trial.

Because the majority of legal battles occur in the pretrial phase, this phase is obviously of great importance. Pretrial issues to be covered here are the

> ➤ selection of an attorney.
> ➤ start of the lawsuit (the complaint).
> ➤ defendant's position (the answer).
> ➤ information gathering (discovery).
> ➤ requests for the court to take action (motions).

Most contractors have an attorney that is used for corporate matters, review of contracts, and real estate transactions, as well as other general practitioner issues. Those attorneys are competent in these areas but are probably not suitable for use in construction litigation. Construction litigation requires an attorney with an understanding of scheduling, change orders, differing site conditions, and other issues unique to the construction industry. You will be distinctly handicapped in court if your attorney does not know the difference between a truss and a joist.

The contractor should interview several attorneys before retaining one. Areas that you might want to question when interviewing an attorney include

> ➤ experience in construction litigation.

> ➤ nonlegal experience in the construction field.

> ➤ memberships in professional legal and construction associations.

> ➤ minimum size of case taken.

> ➤ names of other contractors using this attorney's services.

> ➤ fees charged.

> ➤ method of payment—straight fee or contingency.

Answers to these questions will assist the contractor in determining if the attorney has appropriate experience. Obviously, in large cities, there will be a greater number of construction attorneys than in smaller cities, and the contractor will have to adjust accordingly for the latter.

The lawsuit is officially started when the plaintiff files a complaint in the proper court. In construction cases, parties from the same state will have their case heard in state court. If the parties are from different states and the amount in controversy exceeds $50,000, the case might be brought in the federal court system. Note that, even if the case is brought in federal court, the outcome should be the same because the federal courts are required to follow the laws of the designated state. A local attorney would have a better feel which of the two court systems would be more sympathetic to your case.

For purposes of our discussion, we'll assume that the state court system will be used. If that is the case, the following must be determined in regards to where to file suit:

> ➤ Proper county

> ➤ Proper division within the county

> ➤ Proper branch within the division

The county where the suit is brought is important from a convenience standpoint: a suit brought in a county on the opposite side of the state from where a party resides will be difficult to defend for a party with limited resources. Another less readily apparent reason is that the composition of the inhabitants of a county will most likely reflect the composition of a jury. A jury consisting of people from a certain economic and status group may be more sympathetic to a person of similar status.

The court rules of the state will lay out the choices of which county the suit can be filed in. Suits involving real estate must be filed in the county where the property is located. Suits involving contracts typically must be filed in the county where the defendant resides, where the contract was signed, or where performance of the contract took place.

Once the proper county is chosen, the proper division within the county must be determined. The divisions of the county court system consist of criminal, juvenile, probate, domestic relations, civil, and chancery. Of interest to the contractor are both the civil and chancery divisions.

Chancery courts are set up to hear cases where parties request injunction, and they will most likely hear mechanic's lien cases. Civil courts will hear contract and tort cases.

After choosing the proper division of the county court, the appropriate branch within the division must be determined. An example of the breakdown could be as follows:

➤ Small claims (under $2000)

➤ Medium claims (between $2000 and $20,000)

➤ Large claims (in excess of $20,000)

Each branch will have a slight modification of the rules appropriate to the size of the case. Medium and large claims usually are appropriately handled with the use of an attorney. Small claims rules are set up such that the use of an attorney is not necessary.

As previously stated, the suit is officially started when the complaint is filed. The complaint can be handwritten on a preprinted form for small claims cases or can be a multitude of pages for complicated lawsuits and multiple parties. Every complaint will have the name of the plaintiff and defendant listed at the top of the first page. It is extremely important to have the proper name of the defendant. If the status of the business (i.e., corporation, partnerships, or sole proprietorship) of the party is not known, research must be done to determine the proper status of the opposing party. If the complaint is directed at a corporation, naming the owner of the corporation is insufficient; the proper party must be identified.

The complaint lays out the basic facts and lists the elements of the case, in addition to covering the previously discussed jurisdictional issues. For instance, if the plaintiff is alleging that the defendant breached a contract, the plaintiff must state the appropriate elements for formation of the contract as well as the details of the breach. Jurisdictional issues are satisfied by listing the state of residency of the parties. The following is a very simple example of the wording of a complaint for the breach of a construction contract:

❶ The plaintiff is a registered corporation in State X and is doing business in State X.

❷ The defendant is a registered corporation in State X and with corporate headquarters located in the County of Cook.

❸ Plaintiff and defendant executed a valid contract on January 1, 1994, in Chicago, Illinois, located in the County of Cook.

❹ Under the terms of the contract, the plaintiff was to construct a two-story residence on defendant's property at 123 Main Street in Chicago, Illinois, in the County of Cook.

❺ In consideration of the construction performed by plaintiff, defendant was to pay $150,000 upon completion of the project.

❻ Plaintiff completed the construction project on May 1, 1994.

❼ Defendant as of this date has not paid any of the money due the contractor and is in breach of contract.

❽ Plaintiff requests that the court order defendant to pay $150,000 to plaintiff for services performed and all court costs associated with this action.

Numbers 1 and 2 of the sample complaint list the state of residence of the plaintiff and defendant, which lays out the jurisdiction of the parties. If the defendant is not a resident of the state where the case is filed, the state court might not have proper jurisdiction to hear the case.

As discussed previously in this chapter, the county where the case is filed has important tactical implications. Item 2 lists the location of the defendant's main office because that's a county where the defendant is located and suit may be brought.

To allege a contract, you must first show the existence of the contract. A contract is valid if there was offer, acceptance, and consideration. Item 3 states that there was a contract, the contract is valid, implying that offer, acceptance, and consideration have been satisfied.

Items 4 and 5 list the respective duties of the two parties. The contractor was obligated to construct a two-story residence, and the owner was to pay the contractor $150,000 upon completion. Item 6 states that the contractor has fulfilled the obligation stated in Item 4. Item 7 provides that the owner has not fulfilled the obligation stated in Item 5 and has therefore breached the contract.

Item 8, the request for damages, is one of the most important parts of the complaint. The request for damages basically tells the judge what you are requesting from the defendant. This request can be for monetary damages, or that the defendant do something or refrain from doing something. It is important to clearly state in the complaint what the plaintiff is requesting, because a judge might limit your recovery to what was initially requested. If the state where the suit is brought allows for reimbursement of court costs and attorney fees, these costs should also be included in the complaint.

Once the complaint has been completed and signed, it must be filed with the clerk of the court. The complaint will be delivered to the defendant by a process server, or in small claims cases it may be permitted to serve the defendant by certified mail.

Upon receiving the complaint, the defendant must respond to the allegations. This response is appropriately called an *answer*. The defendant must address *every* item specified in the complaint. Items that are not appropriately addressed by the defendant are deemed to be admitted to be true. The following is an answer to the sample complaint that was discussed earlier in this chapter. (Note the one-to-one correspondence of the answer to the items in the complaint.)

❶ Defendant has insufficient knowledge to answer allegations No. 1 in the complaint.

❷ Defendant admits allegations No. 2.

❸ Defendant denies allegation No. 3.

❹ Defendant denies allegation No. 4.

❺ Defendant denies allegation No. 5.

❻ Defendant denies allegation No. 6.

❼ Defendant denies allegation No. 7.

❽ Defendant requests that this case be dismissed on the grounds that there has been no breach of contract and award defendant court costs and reasonable attorney's fees.

The defendant's response to Item No. 1 of the complaint is given in Item No. 1 of the answer. The defendant has stated that they have insufficient information to determine the business status of the plaintiff because they are not privy to this information. On the other hand, the defendant can answer, and does admit, its own corporate status in Item No. 2.

The defendant in this example has taken the position that there never was a valid contract. Therefore, the defendant has denied the truth of items No. 3 through 7. In keeping with this defense, the defendant has requested in Item 8 that the case be dismissed and court costs be reimbursed to defendant by plaintiff.

After completing the answer to the complaint, the defendant signs the document, files it with the clerk of the circuit court, and sends a copy to the plaintiff. Although the parties may send legal documents directly to each other, they must file a copy of the document with the clerk of the circuit court with proof that it was given to the other party. The clerk of the court files will keep the official and complete record of the case.

The defendant must answer the complaint and file it with the clerk within a certain time period. In the event that the defendant does not meet the deadline, the judge may consider the failure to answer a default. If it is considered a default, the issue in the case will be limited to determining how much the plaintiff should be awarded. Needless to say, a prompt answer is extremely important.

After the answer to the complaint has been filed, the parties should have a basic understanding of the opposing parties' position. But reviewing the complaint and answer presented in this chapter provides little insight into the details of the plaintiff's and defendant's position; and with this limited knowledge, it would be nearly impossible to reach any type of settlement, making the trial full of surprises for both parties. To avoid these problems, the court allows *discovery*.

Discovery is a procedure governed by court rules by which parties can find out information about the opposition's case. Discovery allows you to probe, within limit, into what facts the opposing party knows, and their perception of the case.

The courts provide for and encourage discovery because if opposing parties receive pertinent information, they can better assess their case—which might then promote a settlement and thereby avoid a trial. Even if there is a trial, it might be possible to limit the issues and thus allow for a quicker trial.

Let's examine four types of discovery:

➤ Interrogatories

➤ Request to Produce

➤ Deposition

➤ Request to Admit

Interrogatories are written questions submitted to the opposing party which must be answered under oath. Sample interrogatories questions are to identify

➤ all change orders that were issued with respect to the subject project.

➤ the person or persons in charge of on-site construction supervision.

➤ all construction diaries, logs, and all other written observations for the subject project.

The answers to the interrogatories serve several purposes. First, they provide information about factual issues in the case, including names of witnesses, information contained in field documents, dates of when certain events occurred, etc. Second, it provides information regarding other parties that should be made included in the lawsuit but were unknown to the plaintiff. Third, because the interrogatories must be answered under oath, the position of the opposing party can be determined and used to impeach them if they change positions later in the lawsuit.

Interrogatories must be of a form that can be reasonably answered. If the answer to an interrogatory would take a considerable amount of time to assemble, the court might not require the party to answer. Also, there typically is a limit to the number of questions that can be asked.

Another discovery tool is the *request to produce*. Opposing parties can receive copies of or view documents pertaining to the case. A request to produce may ask the opposing side to provide the following:

➤ All design drawings used for the project

➤ All invoices and other documents pertaining to ordering of material

➤ A copy of all contracts between you and all subcontractors

➤ All documents pertaining to property liability insurance

Note that there is not unlimited access to defendant's files. Certain items regarding the client-attorney privilege are not discoverable.

Depositions are a useful tool for determining your opponent's position on the disagreement. A deposition is an oral interview given under oath. The deposition is conducted by the opposing party's attorney. The party being deposed may also have attorney present. The deposition is recorded and transcribed by a court reporter to provide a permanent record of the deposition. Depositions serve the same purpose as interrogatories, and have the advantage that the witness or party being deposed must answer spontaneously, whereas interrogatories can be answered after spending significant amount of time reviewing the answer before it is submitted to the opposition. However, depositions take time and cost money.

A deposition is typically held at a place that is convenient for the witness to be deposed. Neither the judge or any other court personnel is present during the deposition.

The last type of discovery is the *request to admit*. This technique involves providing the opposing party with a set of written questions that must be answered with a denial or be admitted. These differ from interrogatories in that the request to admit is not seeking information but is seeking admissions; its purpose is to reduce the time and cost of litigation. The following are samples of what could be asked in a request to admit:

> ➢ Admit that the construction was to be performed in accordance with local building codes

> ➢ Admit that the structure collapsed on August 1, 1994

> ➢ Admit that the construction of the building was completed on May 1, 1994

The opposing party must deny, admit, or object to the request to admit. Note that in the event that a party denies a request to admit and it is later proven that the answer should have been admitted, the court may order sanctions and reimbursement costs.

 # Summary

Due to the complexity of construction and the propensity for filing lawsuits, it is not uncommon for a contractor to be sued.

The contractor should take an active role in any litigation.

Most lawsuits never make it to trial and are settled in the pretrial stage.

The contractor should interview attorneys before deciding on the appropriate attorney for the case. Questions should include information on fees and experience.

The lawsuit is initiated by the plaintiff filing a complaint. The defendant must respond to the allegations with what is called the *answer*.

Discovery is a judicially sanctioned process whereby the parties can obtain pertinent information known by the other side. There are several types of discovery techniques which include

- ➤ Interrogatories
- ➤ Depositions
- ➤ Request to admit
- ➤ Request to produce

174

13

Trial

Adverse parties have many opportunities to exit the path that leads to a trial. A disagreement that has proceeded to the point where a trial is necessary has failed to be resolved through various levels of negotiations. These negotiations have occurred between the parties themselves, between the attorneys, and in most situations have failed to reach settlement through court-ordered negotiations. After all of these opportunities to settle the dispute have failed, the parties must posture themselves for trial.

The general public has an understanding of how a trial operates, despite not having any actual involvement in a trial. However, their knowledge has not come from participation but has rather come from exposure to fictional and nonfictional trials shown in movies and on television.

The participants in the trial forum are

Judge An appointed or elected individual responsible for determining what the applicable law is for a given case. If the trial is not making use of a jury, the judge will also be responsible for deciding what the facts of the case are.

Jury A group of unbiased peers of the litigants responsible for deciding what the facts of the case are. The jury, unlike the judge, cannot make decisions of law. The jury will take what they believe to be the facts and reach a verdict that is in accordance with the laws.

Clerk of the Court The clerk who is typically seated next to the judge and who is the administrative aid to the court. Scheduling, paperwork, and other routine matters that are under the jurisdiction of the judge are handled by the clerk.

Bailiff The bailiff acts as the sheriff of the courtroom, to keep oral disputes from turning physical.

The length of a trial is a function of its complexity, as well as the amount of money that is at stake. Construction-related trials typically take from one day to five days to be completed, although in some cases they can last for several months.

The general schedule for a trial is as follows:

❶ Stipulations

❷ Jury selection

❸ Opening statements

❹ Examination of witnesses

❺ Closing statements

Stipulations

A stipulation is an agreement at the start of trial between opposing attorneys to not dispute a certain fact. For example, the parties may stipulate that a building collapsed on January 1, 1990. This stipulation will help reduce the amount of time needed for trial and provides a more economical judicial system.

Jury selection

The constitution provides a right of the parties to have their peers (i.e., jury) decide their case. If neither party desires this option, the case can be decided by the judge. Various issues must be considered before deciding if a jury is an appropriate choice:

➤ Will the use of a jury elongate the trial?

➤ Will a jury be more sympathetic to your case or your opponents?

➤ Is it worth spending the extra money, although it is minimal, in getting a jury trial?

➤ Will the makeup and background of the jury pool be similar to yours or the opponents?

➤ Will having a jury complicate matters?

The pool of jurors is assembled randomly from voter's lists, driver's license lists, etc. The jurors are interviewed individually and, if they satisfy criteria, are added to the jury until the required number is obtained.

The judge will typically allow the jurors to be questioned (called *voire dire*) by the attorneys to determine if there is a reason that it would be inappropriate to have that person on the jury. Other times, the judge may do *voire dire* without allowing the attorneys to ask questions. The areas that prospective jurors are questioned on will depend on the nature of the case. Areas that may be of interest for *voire dire* are as follows:

> ➤ Has the juror ever had any dealings with plaintiff or defendant?

> ➤ Is the juror an employee in the construction industry?

> ➤ What lawsuits has the juror been personally involved in?

> ➤ Will the juror agree to listen to the case and decide it in accordance with the laws?

Any particular answer might not necessarily disqualify the prospective juror, but it does provide insight into how the juror might act.

If the plaintiff or defendant believes that the prospective juror might be prejudiced against them or that the person might not provide a fair decision, they can request the judge to forbid this person from becoming a member of the jury. The attorney must persuade the judge that the prospective juror would be an inappropriate choice.

The parties are also allowed to have a certain limited number of objections to certain prospective jurors that cannot be questioned by the judge. These preemptive moves are very limited and the attorney must use them wisely. When utilizing this objection, the attorney merely states to the judge that the prospective juror is unacceptable. As long as the party has not exceeded their allotted objections, they need not be required to persuade the judge.

Jury selection is a very important part of the trial. In high profile lawsuits, it is not uncommon to have the attorneys hire specialists in jury-selection techniques.

Opening statements

The trial begins with both parties presenting their opening statements; customarily, the plaintiff goes first.

The opening statement gives the litigants their first chance to tell their version of what has occurred. The attorney will lay out for the jury what they can expect to hear in the rest of the trial and how these things will support a verdict in favor of attorney's clients.

It is not too difficult to imagine that some jurors might decide the case on the first impression given by the attorney from the opening statement. An attorney must perform well during all stages of the trial, but a poor opening statement could doom the case from the start.

An effective opening statement must present the party's side of the case from the beginning of the problem to the end and must be detailed enough that a jury will understand the party's position. But it must not be too detailed, or the jury will be overcome by boredom or overwhelmed with information. Finding a balance between these two is difficult and can only be learned from experience.

The items that are covered in the opening statement for a construction case can include the following:

➤ Brief overview of problem

➤ Type of structure in question

➤ Plaintiff's involvement

➤ Defendant's involvement

➤ What went wrong

➤ Who is responsible

➤ What is being requested

➤ Summary

Construction lawsuits most likely will involve some very technical issues. If the jury has difficulty grasping these issues, it is unlikely they will provide a favorable verdict. The attorney can only be effective if the technical issues are presented in a clear, simple, and concise manner.

The opening statement is a good opportunity to do some damage control. If it is anticipated that the opposing party has some evidence that might adversely affect the case, one should consider damage control by mentioning it in the opening statement. For example, let's assume that a contractor builds an addition for $50,000 for Bernice and completes it four days after the promised completion date, but Bernice refuses to pay any of the $50,000. The attorney for the contractor can expect that the attorney for Bernice will make an issue out of the late completion date. For the sake of damage control, it could be wise for the contractor's attorney to admit in the opening statement that the client did not finish the project on schedule. This admission will steal the thunder from the opening statement of the defendant and result in less emphasis being placed on the missed completion date. In most cases, it's much better that the jury hears from your attorney about unpleasant matters than to have them dramatically presented by the opposition.

Direct examination

Each party will be allowed to present their witnesses and their corresponding testimony to the jury. The plaintiff will present all witnesses, and when finished, the defendant will do likewise. When a party presents their own witnesses to testify, it is called *direct examination*. When an attorney is confronting the opposition's witness, it is called *cross-examination*.

The purpose of a direct examination is to get the witness to tell facts that bolster the questioning attorney's case. The attorney will ask the witnesses questions for the purpose of assisting the witnesses in telling what happened.

Witnesses for both sides of the case will often have conflicting versions of the same circumstances; therefore, witness's credibility is almost always at issue. In an effort to make their witnesses credible, attorneys will begin direct examination by eliciting questions on the background of the witness to offer to the jury that the witness is believable.

Cross-examination

An attorney is always given an opportunity to question the other party's witnesses. The purpose of the cross-examination is to bring out any inconsistencies, untruths, or uncertainties in the testimony of the witness.

The demeanor of the attorney will be different for cross-examination than for direct examination. In direct examination, the attorney is dealing with their own witness for the purpose of letting the witnesses tell their version of the facts. Questions during direct examination are general and cannot lead the witness. Cross-examination is the total opposite because the attorney is confronting the witness rather than eliciting a story. The attorney's demeanor will be confrontational in nature, and questions are asked that typically yield only yes or no responses.

The previous chapter discussed the prelitigation portion of disputes. In that chapter, the depositions were discussed as one of the available discovery tools. Most likely, every witness testifying at trial has previously given a deposition on the case. For this reason, the testimony at trial should provide no surprises because the attorneys know the opinions of the witnesses from the depositions. If the witnesses change stories at trial, the attorney can impeach the witness's testimony by use of the earlier deposition testimony. Impeaching a witness during cross-examination is an art. If an attorney finds a flaw in the testimony of the witness, the attorney will bring attention to this flaw to damage the credibility of the testimony of the witness.

Expert witness

Lawyers will often obtain one or more expert witnesses to support their case. An expert witness is a person with a specialized knowledge in his or her profession. This specialized knowledge can be obtained through education, experience, or a combination of both. A person that qualifies as an expert witness can give opinion testimony on the subject matter, whereas a typical witness can only testify to facts within their knowledge.

Closing arguments

After the main portion of the trial is completed, the attorneys need to wrap up the trial with closing arguments. Closing arguments are the last chance that the attorneys will have to sway the jury to accept their position. A closing argument is not much different than the opening statement, except that an opening statement takes the approach of "What you will see from the testimony is that . . ." rather than the "What you heard from the testimony is that . . ." approach used for the closing statement.

Evidence

This completes the overview of the itinerary of a trial, except for one trial-process topic that leads to the greatest number of problems and was not covered due to its complexity: the issue of what evidence either party can present to the jury. The remainder of this chapter is devoted to the subject of evidence.

A piece of evidence, be it a smoking gun, an incriminating document, or a statement that admits guilt, can make or break a case. If the evidence does not get to be known by the jury, the outcome of the case might be totally different than if the evidence was admitted. The determination of the admissibility of evidence is a two-step process. First, the evidence must be relevant to the case at issue; second, there must not be any legal objections to the admission of the evidence to the jury.

Evidence is considered relevant if it concerns the present litigation and offers a fact of some value that will aid in deciding the outcome of the case. For example, if a person were on trial for a crime, would evidence that the parents of this person are in prison for unrelated offenses be relevant? This information is not admissible because it isn't relevant to the present case, nor does it provide any facts that will help decide the case.

Some circumstances will allow "unrelated" evidence to be considered, however:

> **Industry custom.** Standards of the industry may be offered as evidence to show that a party is negligent for deviating from the normal standard of care.

> **Habit.** Evidence of habit can be admitted if it is relevant to prove that the actions of a person on a particular occasion were in conformity with that person's habits.

> **Evidence of business routine.** Evidence that a particular company has an established routine is relevant to show that an event most likely occurred.

These three items address the case where the evidence offered would normally not be considered relevant because it consists of facts outside the current litigation. The court allows this information as evidence because it has some benefit in determining the truth. On the contrary, there are situations where the offered evidence is very relevant and useful for deciding fault but is not admitted for reasons of public policy. The following three items are examples of evidence that is relevant but not admissible:

> The fact that a person has liability insurance, although relevant, is inadmissible to show a person has the resources to pay damages. The jury will not be told which (if any) of the defendants has liability insurance. The courts take this position to avoid juries awarding damages based on which party can afford damages rather than on guilt.

➤ Offers to compromise to settle the dispute will not be allowed as evidence. A defendant may be willing to offer the plaintiff a settlement to drop the suit as a matter of practicality, despite the defendant's opinion of no liability. A jury that is told of a settlement offer made by the defendant may erroneously assume the defendant is guilty.

➤ Information on subsequent repairs is also inadmissible. If the jury is told that, since the time of the accident, the defendant has repaired the alleged dangerous condition, the jury might assume that the defendant must have been negligent. To avoid this situation, a defendant might not repair a possibly dangerous condition until after trial. Allowing such information would indirectly discourage the defendant from making repairs.

A person who has knowledge of certain facts in a case can be subpoenaed and required to testify about these facts. There are privileges that permit a person to refuse to provide this testimonial evidence. Two types of privileges not to testify are as follows:

➤ **Attorney/Client privilege.** The conversations between an attorney and the attorney's client need not be disclosed if the client so desires. Providing the protection of their communications will allow the client to be totally frank and honest with the attorney. Note that disclosures made to the attorney with other parties present takes away this privilege.

➤ **Husband/Wife privilege.** Confidential communications made in reliance upon the bonds of a marital relationship are privileged from disclosure. Therefore, the spouses do not have to disclose any confidential communications made to each other.

The last topic covered here on evidence is the hearsay rule. *Hearsay* is a statement made by someone other than the witness that is being repeated by the witness to prove something is true. Consider the following testimony by a witness:

"When I arrived at the scene of the car accident, Jean told me that the red car went through the red light."

This statement is hearsay and should not be admitted as evidence. It is a statement made by Jean that the witness testifying is now repeating to prove that the red car did not stop at the red light.

Courts will not allow hearsay statements to be used as evidence because the truthfulness of the statement is questionable. In the sample hearsay statement, we do not know anything about Jean. Is she color-blind? Where was she standing at the time of the accident? (Etc.) Unless Jean is brought in to testify, the truthfulness of this statement cannot be tested.

Another example of a statement that could be hearsay is the following testimony of a witness:

"Mick said to me, 'Deliver this box of specially ordered anchor bolts to the contractor today.'"

If the witness delivered a closed unmarked box, the witness would have no idea as to what was in the box; Mick could have filled the box with nails instead of bolts. Therefore, what was in the box could be hearsay and not admissible as evidence.

These two examples are very simple cases of an extremely complicated topic. Nevertheless, they should give the reader a general idea of what hearsay is. It is important to understand that hearsay evidence is disqualified not because the truthfulness of the witness testifying is in question (the veracity of the witness can be determined when the witness is testifying). No, hearsay is not allowed because the truthfulness of the person *being quoted* is in question. In the previous example, the witness may be repeating word for word what Mick said, but it is not known if Mick was revealing truthfully what was in the box.

As with all rules, there are exceptions to the hearsay rule. Even though the witness is repeating what someone else said, sometimes the court is willing to allow the repeated statement in as evidence. The court allows this bending of the rules under the condition that there is some way to assess the truthfulness of the statement being offered. A few of the many exceptions to the hearsay rule are

➤ Statements to a treating physician

➤ Excited utterance

➤ Dying declaration

Statements that are made to a physician for the purposes of treatment are not excluded as hearsay. Therefore, the testimony of the doctor in the following statement is admissible:

"Mary told me she had excruciating pain in her head that often caused her to faint."

Even though the doctor is repeating the statement of Mary, it will be admitted as evidence because it is an exception to the hearsay rule. The court allows this exception because a person seeking treatment from a physician has a motive to tell the truth.

Statements that are made while under the stress of a startling event are also admissible as an exception to the hearsay rule. An example of this, called the *excited utterance exception*, is as follows:

During construction of a high-rise building, Anthony drops a heavy tool that hits Jack who is working on the floor below. When Anthony sees how badly Jack has been injured, he exclaims, "How could I have been so stupid not to hold my tools tight?"

A bystander may testify at trial that Anthony said this because the nature of this startling event would have precluded Anthony from making a fabricated statement.

The last example of exceptions to the hearsay rule—the dying declaration—is based on the allowance that a witness can only repeat the statement if the person being quoted is unavailable to testify at court. Remember, this exception can only be used if the person who made the statement is unavailable to testify.

"When the police arrived at Jack's house, he was bleeding profusely from a gun shot wound and was near death. He meekly muttered the words "Gus did me in.""

If Jack dies or for some other reason became unavailable to testify at trial, this statement would not be treated as hearsay, allowing a bystander to repeat the statement in court. The courts take the position that a person who is facing death has little motive to lie.

 # Summary

A stipulation is an agreement at the start of trial between opposing attorneys to not dispute a certain fact.

Either parties have a right to a jury but should consider the consequence of the use of a jury.

The opening statement is the litigant's first chance to tell their version of what has occurred. The attorney will lay out to the jury what they can expect to hear in the rest of the trial.

The items that are covered in an opening statement of a construction case can include

> a brief overview of problem.

> the type of structure in question.

> the plaintiff's involvement.

> the defendant's involvement.

> what went wrong.

> who is responsible.

> what is being requested.

> the summary.

When a party questions its own witnesses at trial it is called direct examination.

The purpose of direct examination is to get the witness to tell facts that bolster the questioning attorney's case.

When an attorney is questioning the opposing party's witness, it is called *cross-examination*.

Cross-examination is for the purpose of questioning the witness's version of what happened or to discredit the witness.

Closing arguments are for the purpose of summing up the trial.

Evidence is admissible if it is relevant. Evidence is considered relevant if it concerns the present litigation and offers a fact of some value that will help in deciding the outcome of the case.

Evidence may be considered relevant despite the fact that it is not directly related to the litigation at hand (industry custom, habit, and evidence of business routine).

In some cases, the evidence may be relevant but because of public policy reasons is excluded anyway (e.g., liability insurance, settlement offer, subsequent repairs).

Communication between two people might not be admissible because it is privileged information (attorney/client privilege or husband/wife privilege).

Hearsay is a statement made by someone other than the testifying witness that is being repeated by the witness to prove something is true. Hearsay testimony is not permitted unless some exception to the rule allows for it.

Courts will allow hearsay testimony if it fits into one of a few exceptions, some of them being

> ➤ a statement to a treating physician

> ➤ excited utterance

> ➤ dying declaration

14

Property

It is not uncommon for homebuilders to purchase a piece of property, construct a home on it, and search for a buyer after completion. This scenario results in the homebuilder being both a builder and a landowner. As a landowner, it would be useful for the homebuilder to be knowledgeable in regards to easements, deeds, land zoning, title to property, title insurance, and liability (to name a few). Covering all these necessary topics isn't possible because it would require a book in itself. In fact, if you are involved or intend to get involved in significant purchases of property, you should obtain a real estate law text book for an in-depth understanding. Even though this book will not make an in-depth presentation of property law, it will cover what I consider the bare essentials—easements, deeds, and land zoning.

An *easement* is a right acquired by a person or entity to use the land of another for a special purpose. An easement comes into being by a variety of methods, some of which are express agreement, necessity, and prescription.

Before discussing how easements come into being, you should note the difference between a license and an easement because these two can often be confused. A *license* is the allowing of temporary access to property, such as granting a landscaping company temporary access in order to cut the grass; it's more personal in nature and doesn't pass with the sale of the land. An *easement*, on the other hand, is a more permanent arrangement and is transferred with the property when it is sold.

Easement

An easement can be created by an express grant, which must be in writing, describe the easement, and be signed. Typical types of easements include the burying of utilities, access to the property for repair of utilities, and allowing vehicles to pass over the property.

An *easement by necessity* is not created by any written agreements but comes into existence as a matter of practicality. This easement is created by law when a piece of property is sold that has no way of access onto public property. Under these circumstances, the users of the land-locked piece of property will be granted egress to roads by an easement of necessity over the adjacent property.

The final type of easement to be discussed is an *easement by prescription*. An easement acquired by prescription is the right to use a piece of property that is acquired by the lapse of time. For example, if a person has been crossing over a piece of property for a long period of time (20 to 30 years), they may be granted an easement by prescription to continue this use.

These three types of easements are only an overview of the topic; if you have concerns about possible easement problems, you should consult a lawyer.

 # Deeds

A deed is a written document by which ownership of land is transferred. The most common types of deeds are warranty and quit claim.

A *warranty deed* guarantees that the deed being transferred to the purchaser will meet a certain standard, including that the person selling the property is the actual owner, that there are no liens on the property, and that no other person has any claims against the property. If it is later found that these standards have not been met, the purchaser can sue for the failure of the seller to provide the proper deed.

A *quit claim deed* guarantees nothing. The person who is selling the property is basically stating that they believe they own the property but cannot guarantee that others might not think they also own it. This deed is used when the seller does not know whether the deed they have is good or bad.

Zoning

Many projects die a slow death while the general contractor tries to obtain a land-zoning change or tries to get the necessary permits. Poor planning by the general contractor, and delays by overworked building departments, result in more time spent seeking a permit than it takes to construct the house. Requests for land-zoning changes can be equally frustrating as time slips away and legal costs accumulate.

The general contractor must be knowledgeable in land zoning when building an entire subdivision, when the project is conditioned on a zoning change, or when the contractor is purchasing a parcel of land and selling the house and land as one package. The various land-zoning issues presented in this chapter are as follows:

➤ The zoning ordinance

➤ Spot zoning

➤ Conditional zoning

➤ Variances

➤ Special use

➤ Nonconforming use

➤ Aesthetic zoning

➤ Planned Unit Development

The zoning ordinance

The zoning ordinance divides a city into different land-zoning districts. Each land-zoning district will place similar land parcels in similar areas into the same classification. The number of classifications depends on the variety of businesses, population density, and common land use in the area. Here's a sample of the possible classifications that could be used in a suburban setting:

R1   Single family residential district
R2   Single family residential district

R3   Residential transition district
R4   Multi-family residential district
C1   Limited commercial and office district
C2   Shopping center district
C3   Highway commercial district
I   Industrial district
AG Agriculture district

The zoning ordinance should be consulted for each city because the designations and terminology might have different meanings. The allowable uses for the classifications listed here may be as follows:

✳ **R1: Single family residential**
This district is designed to provide for a low-density living environment. Only single-family detached dwellings are permitted in this district.

✳ **R2: Single family residential**
This district is designed to allow for large lots. Only single-family detached dwellings are permitted in this district.

✳ **R3: Residential transition**
This district is designed to provide for a medium-density living environment. Structures are limited to single-family detached, two-family dwellings, and townhouses.

✳ **R4: Multi-family residential**
This district is designed for a planned mixture of residential dwellings limited to 10 dwellings per acre.

✳ **C1: Limited commercial & office**
This district is limited to small commercial and office buildings including bookstores, florist shops, gift shops, ice cream shops, and similar office uses including architect's offices, insurance agencies, newspaper offices, employment agencies, and similar businesses.

✳ **C2: Shopping center**
This district is designed for large neighborhood shopping centers. Shopping center use includes carpet stores, department stores, drugstores, toy stores, television sales, shoe stores, and similar businesses.

✳ **C3: Highway commercial**

This district is designed to provide a variety of commercial facilities. Highway commercial use shall include automobile sales and services, appliance stores, veterinary clinics, medical clinics, real estate offices, and similar businesses.

✳ **I: Industrial**

This district is designed for warehouse, office, and research activity. Industrial districts include contractor offices, book keeping services, testing and research offices, laboratories, and restaurants.

✳ **AG: Agriculture**

This district is designed for farming use.

Spot zoning

The governing body of a locale provides a zoning scheme that reasonably divides the property into different zoning classifications. Each classification consists of the grouping of very similar adjacent parcels of land. It is not surprising that some individuals will later request that the parcel of land be rezoned for a more advantageous use. Such a zoning change is welcomed so the highest and best use of the land is obtained, provided that the change is in line with the overall zoning scheme. A change that results in zoning that is not in harmony with the overall plan is called spot zoning. If 50 parcels of property are zoned for residential development and one is rezoned for heavy industry, spot zoning may be occurring. A zoning change is considered spot zoning if it is a drastic change not in accordance with the overall plan, and affects a small parcel of land for the benefit of only the parcel owner. Spot zoning will be prohibited by the court since allowing such a change undermines the zoning system, detrimentally affecting adjacent landowners and inviting graft.

Conditional zoning

Spot zoning is an outright, no strings attached, zoning change. In contrast, conditional zoning is a rezoning of a piece of property with a requirement that something be done before the zoning change is allowed. For example, a general contractor may desire to build multi-family homes on land zoned for single family use. The zoning board may grant the change on the condition that the existing streets in the neighborhood be widened to accommodate the increased traffic. Such conditional zoning is frowned upon by the courts since it invites "behind closed door" deals and there is no established criteria for allowing the change.

Variances

Allowing a parcel of land to have different zoning classifications than similar adjacent property is in violation of a fair zoning ordinance. However, to effectively function, the zoning laws must have at least some flexibility. Spot zoning and conditional zoning are changes given by the zoning board just for the purpose of a more advantageous classification. A variance, on the other hand, allows for a more advantageous classification because the owner has a unique problem.

Variances are of two types: *use* and *area*. The use variance allows the parcel to be used in a manner inconsistent with the zoning ordinance, while the area variance allows for the relaxation of physical dimensioning requirements (minimum house size, minimum distance from roadway, etc.). A variance is only allowed if the three following requirements are satisfied:

> ➤ Present zoning results in an unnecessary hardship to the owner.

> ➤ The problem is unique to this parcel of land.

> ➤ The variance is not totally inconsistent with the overall zoning plan.

You need to plan well when seeking a variance. A variance for a change of use may not allow for a change in area or other needed variance, so it's wise to determine all the needed variances and obtain them all at one time.

Special use

In some cases, a parcel of land will have a zoning classification plus an additional zoning option. For example, a parcel of land may be zoned for single family use, with an option to allow a church, school, or hospital. This additional zoning option is called a *special use*. A special-use zoning request is not a change in zoning but still needs the approval of the zoning board because, although hospitals and schools are beneficial to the public, there are serious ramifications on traffic and adjacent parcels. The special use allows the zoning board to have some control over the land development. Note that the special use is different than a variance, because a variance requires that the owner be suffering a hardship.

Nonconforming use

When an area is zoned for the first time or even when land is rezoned, some of the existing uses of the land will be in conflict with the new zoning ordinance; and elimination of these existing uses would be unwise and unfair. To avoid this problem, the zoning board allows a nonconforming use, which allows the owner to continue to use the land for its current designation, despite the conflict in zoning. The nonconforming use can be for an indeterminate or limited period of time, and the conditions of the zoning relaxation are contingent on the business not being expanded or changed.

Aesthetic zoning

Some municipalities require that approval from an architectural review board be received prior to construction. Although such reviews seem subjective and can possibly lead to abuse, this decision has been upheld by the courts.

Planned Unit Development (PUD)

A PUD differs from the typical zoning scheme. A typical zoning ordinance places many land parcels into one zoning classification, but a PUD takes the same group of parcels while allowing several zoning classifications. This gives the group of parcels the flexibility to have single family, multi-family, and light commercial interspersed to form a more diverse and convenient neighborhood.

A
Residential construction contract sample

This appendix contains a sample construction contract. The contract beginning on the next page is only a sample and is not meant to be used unless an attorney is consulted to explain and make the necessary modifications. The authors and publisher are not responsible for the unauthorized use of this sample contract. Any party using this appendix agrees to hold the authors and publisher harmless for any and all causes of action.

Residential Construction Contract

Purchaser:

Address:

Phone:

General Contractor:

Address:

Phone:

The general contractor agrees to construct a _____-style home with basement and garage, subject to the terms and conditions of this contract, at _____, whose legal description is:

The purchaser agrees to purchase the residence at this address under the terms and conditions of this contract.

Contract documents

The following items are hereby included as part of this contract:

➤ Design drawings: Title:
  Prepared by:

➤ Attached specifications

➤ Local building codes

➤ Occupational Safety and Health Act (OSHA) requirements

➤ Local fire codes

➤ All applicable material codes

In the event contract documents conflict, the order of precedence shall be as just listed.

Property ownership   The purchaser represents that the property is solely and exclusively theirs. The purchaser further represents that the property is free and clear of all liens and encumbrances unless noted elsewhere in this contract.

Taxes & assessments   The purchaser and general contractor shall each pay their pro-rata share of real estate taxes and assessments for the year of closing at the time of closing. The estimated real estate taxes for the year of proration shall be based on 105% of the previous year. The general contractor shall pay any taxes accrued prior to the year of closing.

Purchase price and payouts

Base Amount $
Extras $
Total $

Schedule of payments

(i) At contract signing

(ii) House under roof

(iii) Interior ready for paint

(iv) Completion

Loan commitment   The purchaser must receive a loan commitment within 30 days from signing of this contract in the amount of $_____. The purchaser shall make every reasonable effort to obtain the loan commitment and shall pay all usual and customary charges imposed by the lending institution. The purchaser shall provide a copy of the commitment letter to the general contractor within the 30 days. If the purchaser is unable to obtain financing, the purchaser shall notify the general contractor within the 30 days. If the purchaser notifies the general contractor that a loan commitment cannot be obtained, the general contractor has the option to obtain a loan commitment on behalf of the purchaser.

All associated fees will be paid for by the purchaser. Failure of the general contractor to exercise this option makes this contract null and void.

Permits   The purchaser shall pay all fees for any and all permits required for the project, including the building permit. In the event that the design drawings are not acceptable for the obtaining of a building permit, it shall be the purchaser's responsibility to have the drawings modified as necessary at no cost to the general contractor. Other permits include but are not limited to building, water, sewer, septic, well, and site grading. The general contractor shall be responsible for obtaining the permits.

Testing   The purchaser is responsible for obtaining, as well as paying, all fees for any and all testing needed for construction of the residence. Testing includes, but is not limited to, soil strength analysis, permeability tests, and water quality testing. The general contractor shall arrange for all testing with the exception of the soil test, which shall be arranged by the owner with an analysis received prior to the start of construction.

Time of construction   The structure shall be completed no later than six months from the signing of the contract. The six month period shall be extended for circumstances beyond the control of the general contractor such as, but not limited to labor strikes, material availability, war, natural disasters, and other unforeseen acts of God. The six month period shall be extended by the length of time of the interruption. The general contractor agrees to pay $_____ per day for every day beyond the six months that the structure is not completed. This $_____ is compensation for inconveniences and living costs for the purchaser. The purchaser agrees to close on the house, pay the full purchase price, and receive ownership no later than 14 days after completion.

Quality of work   All work performed by the general contractor and subcontractors hired by the general contractor shall be in accordance with good construction practice, drawings, and specifications. The work shall meet all applicable building codes and be performed in a quality manner. All work shall be free of defects and faults.

Materials   The contractor is required to furnish all material necessary to complete the house. The contractor is the owner of the material, and is therefore responsible for the material until it is installed. The material furnished shall be of good quality, new and at least equal to the quality of the standard in the industry for the respective type of product. The general contractor shall be allowed to substitute material when the specified material is no longer available or is not feasible to purchase. The purchaser shall be notified of such changes and be allowed a reasonable objection to the substitute.

Change orders   Any changes, deviation, or additional work shall only be performed after a change order has been received by the general contractor. The change order shall contain a description of the work, change in price, and the signature of the purchaser. The change order shall be signed by the general contractor if the general contractor agrees to perform the work at the stipulated price. The general contractor shall not have the right to refuse any reasonable change order. In the case where it is not possible to wait for a properly processed change order, the general contractor shall notify the purchaser of the additional work and price for the change in work. The owner shall provide a verbal response and then provide a properly processed change order within four working days.

Purchaser insurance   The purchaser shall obtain and pay for fire insurance with extended coverage and builders risk insurance for joint coverage of the purchaser, general contractor, and subcontractors. The insurance shall be in the amount of the contract price of the structure excluding concrete work items. The purchaser shall furnish the general contractor evidence of this insurance which shall be obtained under the condition that the insurance cannot be cancelled without 30 days notice to the general contractor.

General contractor   The general contractor shall obtain and pay for Comprehensive General Liability Insurance and all other insurance required by law. These insurance requirements include but are not limited to

➤ Workman's compensation

➤ General liability: Personal injury

➤ General liability: Property damage

The general contractor shall provide statutory amounts for insurance required by law and $_____ each person and $_____ each occurrence for general liability insurance. Prior to the start of construction, the general contractor shall provide evidence of the required insurance with a provision that the policy cannot be cancelled without 30 days notice to the purchaser. The policy must cover all material prior to attachment to the structure. All subcontractors employed by the general contractor must maintain insurance in the same amount as required of the general contractor.

Warranty provided by General Contractor

➤ *Alternative 1*   The general contractor warrants all work against defects. The general contractor agrees to correct any defective work at no cost to the purchaser. This warranty is in effect only for one year from the date of completion or date of possession, whichever comes first.

➤ *Warranties provided by statute*   The purchaser is limited to warranties provided by the general contractor as discussed earlier. The general contractor makes no other warranties, express or implied, including, but not limited to, the implied warranty of habitability or merchantability or fitness for a particular purpose.

Safety   The general contractor shall be solely responsible for providing a safe work site. The work site shall be safe for workers and all persons. The general contractor shall be responsible for providing a safe work site and initiating safety programs for all subcontractors. Precautions shall be taken to protect all property. The general contractor is responsible for meeting all federal and state safety requirements including compliance with OSHA regulations.

Subcontractors   The general contractor is responsible for ensuring that all work performed by subcontractors is performed in an acceptable manner and in accordance with the contract, design drawings, and specifications. The general contractor shall not use any subcontractors who are not fully insured as required by this contract or any subcontractor reasonably objected to by the purchaser. The contractor shall not be required to hire any specific subcontractor unless expressly specified in this contract.

Destruction of premises   In the event the structure is destroyed before the purchaser has taken ownership, the general contractor shall choose one of the following options.

Within two weeks of the date of occurrence of the destruction, the general contractor shall:

(i) Rebuild and finish the structure within 180 calendar days using the insurance proceeds, or

(ii) Void the contract, receive the insurance proceeds, and return deposit to purchaser.

Utilities   The general contractor shall be responsible for arranging for permanent utility connections to the residence as well as for the cost incurred to provide utility service to the residence. All costs incurred for utility services prior to the closing shall be paid for by the general contractor. The general contractor shall notify all utility companies prior to any digging to avoid damage to buried service lines.

Clean up   The general contractor shall keep the construction site in a neat and clean condition during the life of this contract regardless if the work is being performed by the general contractor or a subcontractor. All material shall be stored in an orderly, neat, and safe manner. The entire premises, interior and exterior, shall be cleaned immediately prior to closing, including removal of all trash and debris.

Punch list   At the discretion of the general contractor, the purchaser may take possession of the property upon substantial completion of the residence. If the purchaser does take possession a final "punch list" shall be recorded. The punch list shall list with specificity, what work is needed to achieve final completion of the contract. The contractor agrees to work diligently to complete the punch list items within 30 days of possession. However, the general contractor shall be paid in full regardless of the unfinished items on the punch list.

Assignment of contract   This contract cannot be assigned to any other party without prior approval from the nonassigning party.

However, this contract shall be binding upon and be for the benefit of the parties to the agreement, their heirs and successors and personal representatives.

Default   In the event that the contractor fails to carry out the terms of this contract the purchaser shall make a written notice to the contractor of the lack of progress. If the contractor does not respond in 10 working days, the purchaser may terminate the contract. The general contractor shall pay to the purchaser any additional cost beyond the original contract for completion of the structure. In the event the purchaser fails to make a required payment, the contractor shall make a written protest of the missed payment. If the purchaser does not make payment, the contractor may void the contract and receive payment for all work completed. The nonbreaching party shall be compensated for any losses including attorney's fees for the breach.

Entire agreement   This agreement constitutes the entire agreement and is a final complete expression of the agreement between the parties. All prior discussions, promises, or representations are merged into this document.

B
Contract specifications

This appendix contains a sample set of specifications. This appendix is only a sample and is not meant to be used without modification. Any party using this appendix assumes all the risks and agrees to hold the authors and publisher harmless for any and all causes of action.

Excavation   The contractor shall perform the following excavation at the contractor's cost:

> ➤ Removal of tree or bush growth in area of excavation.

> ➤ Strip topsoil and stockpile.

> ➤ All necessary foundation excavating.

> ➤ All necessary foundation backfilling.

> ➤ Spreading of stockpiled soil upon completion of the structure.

The purchaser shall pay the expense for any labor or material for the following items:

➤ Removal of trees or bush growth outside excavation area.

➤ Additional grading beyond spreading of topsoil.

➤ Removal and disposal of any buried items.

Concrete foundations   All footings and foundations shall reach at least _____ psi in 28 days. Steel reinforcing bars shall be _____ in. diameter and installed at locations shown on design drawings.

Steel members   Steel pipe columns shall be _____ in. outside diameter and filled with concrete. The steel pipe columns shall conform to ASTM standards. Steel beams shall be _____ or as specified on the design drawings. Steel beams shall conform to ASTM standards.

Foundation wall dampproofing   All portions of the foundation wall that will be buried below grade shall have a coating of an asphalt based foundation dampproofing on the exterior face. Dampproofing shall be applied when the temperature is above _____ degrees F and no rain or snow will occur within _____ hours. Dampproofing shall consist of two layers applied in opposite directions.

Footing drains   Footing drains shall be a minimum of _____ in. diameter plastic perforated pipe. The pipe shall meet ASTM standards. The drain shall be placed in _____ in. of stone. The footing drain shall empty by gravity away from the structure or into a sump pit.

Fireplace   Fireplaces shall be prefabricated with the size shown on the design drawings. Fireplace design shall be certified by the American Gas Association and have appropriate venting.

Exterior walls   Exterior walls shall be constructed of _____ studs unless noted differently on the drawing. Exterior cladding shall be cedar siding or brick over wood sheathing as shown on the design drawings. A building wrap shall be used between the cladding and the sheathing. Cedar siding shall be stained with two coats.

Interior walls   Interior walls shall be constructed of _____ studs that are _____ in. on center.

Floor and ceiling framing   All wood framing shall be 2 × 8, 2 × 10, 2 × 12 and spaced as noted on the drawings. Wood shall be _____. Joists shall have bracing located between adjacent joists.

Prefabricated wood trusses   Prefabricated trusses shall be designed to carry the appropriate loads. A stamp by a licensed structural engineer shall accompany each truss.

Roofing   Shingles shall be _____ lbs. fiberglass with a one year warranty on labor and a minimum 25-year warranty on the material. Felt under shingles shall be a minimum of _____ pounds. The roofing material shall be secured to _____ in. thick exterior grade plywood.

Gutters and downspouts   All gutters and downspouts shall be ____ in. aluminum-box-type construction.

Windows   All windows shall be casement with aluminum-clad exterior and shall be manufactured by _____ windows or an approved equivalent. Windows shall include screen and storm windows.

Garage doors   All garage doors shall be plain raised redwood panel doors. Redwood doors shall be weather treated.

Septic system   Complete septic shall be installed as per plans, including stone, filter paper, pipe lines, septic tanks and backfilling. All work shall meet county approval.

Driveway   The driveway shall consist of a _____ in. stone base below _____ in. thick asphalt. The stone shall be compacted prior to placing the asphalt.

Concrete slabs   Concrete slabs shall be poured on a minimum of _____ in. of gravel and visqueen. The concrete slabs shall be reinforced with welded wire fabric. The concrete mix shall be such that the strength of the concrete is at least _____ psi within 28 days.

Plumbing   The general contractor shall provide the following:

Water   ➤ Piping for all sink, bathrooms, dishwasher, water heaters, and all other items that require water.

           ➤ ____ gallon hot water heater

           ➤ Well

           ➤ Kitchen sink

           ➤ Utility sink

           ➤ Shower bases

           ➤ Faucets

           ➤ Exterior faucet

           ➤ Sump pumps

           ➤ Water softener

Wastewater   ➤ Piping from all sinks, bathroom, etc.

           ➤ Septic system

Gas   ➤ Gas piping from exterior source to furnaces, stoves, fireplace log lighter, dryer, and water heater

Allowances   Septic $
            Water softener $
            Well $
            Plumbing fixtures $

Heating   Two high efficiency gas burning furnaces with galvanized metal supply ducts shall be sized and installed. The furnace shall be brand or at least of equal quality. Furnace shall be operable by digital thermometer with programming capability.

Insulation   Insulation with the following R number shall be provided.

Ceiling   R =
Walls   R =
Floor   R =

Insulation shall only be provided in garage walls common to living areas. The exterior of the house shall be wrapped with draft reducing plastic.

Paint   Two coats of flat latex paint shall be applied to all walls and ceilings. Colors other than white shall result in an extra charge.

Trim   All interior doors and trim shall be _____. Doors shall be stained and sealed and of the six-panel style. Base trim and door casings as well as any crown moldings specified on drawings shall be provided by the contractor and shall be stained and sealed.

Cabinets   Kitchen cabinets shall be constructed of oak and have minimum 12 in. shelf width. Bathroom cabinets shall have mirror doors and be set into the wall. There is a $_____ allowance for the cabinets.

Stairs   The stairs and handrail for the stairs shall be oak and be sized to meet the applicable codes. The stairs and railing for the basement steps can be either pine or oak.

Finished floors   Ceramic tile shall be installed at the following locations:

➤ Foyer

➤ Kitchen

➤ Dinette

➤ Bathrooms

The allowance for ceramic tile is $ _____.

Carpet shall be installed at the following locations:

➤ Bedrooms

➤ Family room

➤ Office

➤ Living room

➤ Dining room

➤ Stairs

➤ Upstairs hallway

The allowance for carpet is $ _____.

Lighting fixtures   The contractor will install all switches and wiring for lighting fixtures and plug receptacles. The total number of fixtures needed is _____. Fixture allowance is $ _____.

Vanities and countertops   These items will be installed by the contractor with an allowance of $ _____.

Appliances   Contractors shall install the following appliances:

➤ Kitchen range $ allowance

➤ Refrigerator $ allowance

➤ Dishwasher $ allowance

➤ Washer $ allowance

➤ Dryer $ allowance

Air conditioning unit   Contractor shall provide a properly sized air conditioner from _____.

C
Construction Industry Arbitration rules

The following rules are reprinted from the Construction Industry Arbitration rules of the American Arbitration Association.

 ## 1. Agreement of parties

The parties shall be deemed to have made these rules a part of their arbitration agreement whenever they have provided for arbitration by the American Arbitration Association (hereinafter AAA) or under its Construction Industry Arbitration Rules. These rules and any amendment of them shall apply in the form existing at the time the demand for arbitration or submission agreement is received by the

AAA. The parties, by written agreement, may vary the procedures set forth in these rules.

2. Name of tribunal

Any tribunal constituted by the parties for the settlement of their dispute under these rules shall be called the Construction Industry Arbitration Tribunal.

3. Administrator & delegation of duties

When parties agree to arbitrate under these rules, or when they provide for arbitration by the AAA and an arbitration is initiated under these rules, they thereby authorize the AAA to administer the arbitration. The authority and duties of the AAA are prescribed in the agreement of the parties and in these rules, and may be carried out through such of the AAA's representatives as it may direct.

4. National Panel of Arbitrators

In cooperation with the National Construction Dispute Resolution Committee, the AAA shall establish and maintain a National Panel of Construction Industry Arbitrators and shall appoint arbitrators therefrom as hereinafter provided.

5. Regional offices

The AAA may, in its discretion, assign the administration of an arbitration to any of its regional offices.

6. Initiation under an arbitration provision in a contract

Arbitration under an arbitration provision in a contract shall be initiated in the following manner:

(a) The initiating party (hereinafter claimant) shall, within the time period, if any, specified in the contract(s), give written notice to the other party (hereinafter respondent) of its intention to arbitrate (demand), which notice shall contain a statement setting forth the nature of the dispute, the amount involved, if any, the remedy sought, and the hearing locale requested, and

(b) Shall file at any regional office of the AAA three copies of the notice and three copies of the arbitration provisions of the contract, together with the appropriate administrative fee as provided in the Administrative Fee Schedule.

The AAA shall give notice of the filing to the respondent or respondents. A respondent may file an answering statement in duplicate with the AAA within ten days after notice from the AAA, in which event the respondent shall at the same time send a copy of the answering statement to the claimant. If a counterclaim is asserted, it shall contain a statement setting forth the nature of the counterclaim, the amount involved, if any, and the remedy sought. If a counterclaim is made in the answering statement, the appropriate fee provided in the Administrative Fee Schedule shall be forwarded to the AAA with the answering statement. If no answering statement is filed within the stated time, it will be treated as a denial of the claim. Failure to file an answering statement shall not operate to delay the arbitration.

7. Initiation under a submission

Parties to any existing dispute may commence an arbitration under these rules by filing at any regional office of the AAA three copies of a written submission to arbitrate under these rules, signed by the parties. It shall contain a statement of the matter in dispute, the amount of money involved, if any, the remedy sought, and the hearing locale requested, together with the appropriate administrative fee as provided in the Administrative Fee Schedule.

8. Changes of claim

After filing of a claim, if either party desires to make any new or different claim or counterclaim, same shall be made in writing and filed with the AAA, and a copy shall be mailed to the other party, who shall have a period of ten days from the date of such mailing within which to file an answer with the AAA. After the arbitrator is appointed, however, no new or different claim may be submitted except with the arbitrator's consent.

 # 9. Applicable procedures

Unless the AAA in its discretion determines otherwise, the Expedited Procedures shall be applied in a case where no disclosed claim or counterclaim exceeds $50,000, exclusive of interest and arbitration costs. Parties may also agree to the Expedited Procedures in cases involving claims in excess of $50,000. The Expedited Procedures shall be applied as described in Sections 53 through 57 of these rules, in addition to any other portion of these rules that is not in conflict with the Expedited Procedures.

All other cases shall be administered in accordance with Sections 1 through 52 of these rules.

10. Administrative conference, preliminary hearing, and mediation conference

At the request of any party or at the discretion of the AAA, an administrative conference with the AAA and the parties and/or their representatives will be scheduled in appropriate cases to expedite the arbitration proceedings.

In large or complex cases, at the request of any party or at the discretion of the arbitrator or the AAA, a preliminary hearing with the parties and/or their representatives and the arbitrator may be scheduled by the arbitrator to specify the issues to be resolved, to stipulate to uncontested facts, and to consider any other matters that will expedite the arbitration proceedings. Consistent with the expedited nature of arbitration, the arbitrator may, at the preliminary hearing, establish (i) the extent of and schedule for the production of relevant documents and other information, (ii) the identification of any witnesses to be called, and (iii) a schedule for further hearings to resolve the dispute.

With the consent of the parties, the AAA at any stage of the proceeding may arrange a mediation conference under the Construction Industry Mediation Rules, in order to facilitate settlement. The mediator shall not be an arbitrator appointed to the case. Where the parties to a pending arbitration agree to mediate under the AAA's rules, no additional administrative fee is required to initiate the mediation.

11. Fixing of locale

The parties may mutually agree on the locale where the arbitration is to be held. If any party requests that the hearing be held in a specific locale and the other party files no objection thereto within ten days after notice of the request has been mailed to it by the AAA, the locale shall be the one requested. If a party objects to the locale requested by the other party, the AAA shall have the power to determine the locale and its decision shall be final and binding.

12. Qualifications of an arbitrator

Any neutral arbitrator appointed pursuant to Section 13, 14, 15, or 54, or selected by mutual choice of the parties or their appointees, shall be subject to disqualification for the reasons specified in Section 19. If the parties specifically so agree in writing, the arbitrator shall not be subject to disqualification for those reasons.

Unless the parties agree otherwise, an arbitrator selected unilaterally by one party is a party-appointed arbitrator and is not subject to disqualification pursuant to Section 19.

The term *arbitrator* in these rules refers to the arbitration panel, whether composed of one or more arbitrators and whether the arbitrators are neutral or party appointed.

13. Appointment from panel

If the parties have not appointed an arbitrator and have not provided any other method of appointment, the arbitrator shall be appointed in the following manner: immediately after the filing of the demand or submission, the AAA shall submit simultaneously to each party to the dispute an identical list of names of persons chosen from the panel.

Each party to the dispute shall have ten days from the mailing date in which to cross off any names objected to, number the remaining names in order of preference, and return the list to the AAA. If a party does not return the list within the time specified, all persons named therein shall be deemed acceptable. From among the persons who have been approved on both lists, and in accordance with the designated order of mutual preference, the AAA shall invite the acceptance of an arbitrator to serve. If the parties fail to agree on any of the persons named, or if acceptable arbitrators are unable to act, or if for any other reason the appointment cannot be made from the submitted lists, the AAA shall have the power to make the appointment from among other members of the panel without the submission of additional lists.

14. Direct appointment by a party

If the agreement of the parties names an arbitrator or specifies a method of appointing an arbitrator, that designation or method shall be followed. The notice of appointment, with the name and address of the arbitrator, shall be filed with the AAA by that party. Upon the request of any appointing party, the AAA shall submit a list of members of the panel from which the party may, if it so desires, make the appointment.

If the agreement specifies a period of time within which an arbitrator shall be appointed and any party fails to make the appointment within that period, the AAA shall make the appointment.

If no period of time is specified in the agreement, the AAA shall notify the party to make the appointment. If within ten days thereafter an arbitrator has not been appointed by a party, the AAA shall make the appointment.

 # 15. Appointment of neutral arbitrator by party-appointed arbitrators or parties

If the parties have selected party-appointed arbitrators, or if such arbitrators have been appointed as provided in Section 14, and the parties have authorized them to appoint a neutral arbitrator within a specified time and no appointment is made within that time or any agreed extension thereof, the AAA may appoint the neutral arbitrator, who shall act as chairperson.

If no period of time is specified for appointment of the neutral arbitrator and the party-appointed arbitrators or the parties do not make the appointment within ten days from the date of the appointment of the last party-appointed arbitrator, the AAA may appoint the neutral arbitrator, who shall act as chairperson.

If the parties have agreed that their party appointed arbitrators shall appoint the neutral arbitrator from the panel, the AAA shall furnish to the party-appointed arbitrators, in the manner prescribed in Section 13, a list selected from the panel, and the appointment of the neutral arbitrator shall be made as prescribed in that section.

16. Nationality of arbitrator in international arbitration

Where the parties are nationals or residents of different countries, any neutral arbitrator shall, upon the request of either party, be appointed from among the nationals of a country other than that of any of the parties. The request must be made prior to the time set for the appointment of the arbitrator as agreed by the parties or set by these rules.

 # 17. Number of arbitrators

If the arbitration agreement does not specify the number of arbitrators, the dispute shall be heard and determined by one arbitrator, unless the AAA, in its discretion, directs that a greater number of arbitrators be appointed.

18. Notice to arbitrator of appointment

Notice of the appointment of the neutral arbitrator, whether appointed mutually by the parties or by the AAA, shall be mailed to the arbitrator by the AAA, together with a copy of these rules, and the signed acceptance of the arbitrator shall be filed with the AAA prior to the opening of the first hearing.

19. Disclosure & challenge procedure

Any person appointed as neutral arbitrator shall disclose to the AAA any circumstance likely to affect impartiality, including any bias or any financial or personal interest in the result of the arbitration or any past or present relationship with the parties or their representatives. Upon receipt of such information from the arbitrator or another source, the AAA shall communicate the information to the parties and, if it deems it appropriate to do so, to the arbitrator and others. Upon objection of a party to the continued service of a neutral arbitrator, the AAA shall determine whether the arbitrator should be disqualified and shall inform the parties of its decision, which shall be conclusive.

20. Vacancies

If for any reason an arbitrator is unable to perform the duties of the office, the AAA may, on proof satisfactory to it, declare the office vacant.

Vacancies shall be filled in accordance with the applicable provisions of these rules. In the event of a vacancy in a panel of neutral arbitrators after the hearings have commenced, the remaining arbitrator or arbitrators may continue with the hearing and determination of the controversy, unless the parties agree otherwise.

21. Date, time, & place of hearing

The arbitrator shall set the date, time, and place for each hearing. The AAA shall mail to each party notice thereof at least ten days in advance, unless the parties by mutual agreement waive such notice or modify the terms thereof.

22. Representation

Any party may be represented by counsel or other authorized representative. A party intending to be so represented shall notify the other party and the AAA of the name and address of the representative at least three days prior to the date set for the hearing at which that person is first to appear. When such a representative initiates an arbitration or responds for a party, such notice is deemed to have been given.

23. Stenographic record

Any party desiring a stenographic record shall make arrangements directly with a stenographer and shall notify the other party of these arrangements in advance of the hearing. The requesting party or parties shall pay the cost of the record. If the transcript is agreed by the parties to be, or determined by the arbitrator to be, the official record of the proceeding, it must be made available to the arbitrator and to the other parties for inspection, at a date, time, and place determined by the arbitrator.

24. Interpreters

Any party wishing an interpreter shall make all arrangements directly with the interpreter and shall assume the costs of the service.

25. Attendance at hearings

The arbitrator shall maintain the privacy of the hearings unless the law provides to the contrary.

Any person having a direct interest in the arbitration is entitled to attend hearings. The arbitrator shall otherwise have the power to require the exclusion of any witness, other than a party or other essential person, during the testimony of any other witness. It shall be discretionary with the arbitrator to determine the propriety of the attendance of any other person.

26. Postponements

The arbitrator for good cause shown may postpone any hearing upon the request of a party or upon the arbitrator's own initiative, and shall also grant such postponement when all of the parties agree thereto.

27. Oaths

Before proceeding with the first hearing, each arbitrator may take an oath of office and, if required by law, shall do so. The arbitrator may require witnesses to testify under oath administered by any duly qualified person and, if it is required by law or requested by any party, shall do so.

28. Majority decision

All decisions of the arbitrators must be by a majority. The award must also be made by a majority unless the concurrence of all is expressly required by the arbitration agreement or by law.

29. Order of proceedings and communication with arbitrator

A hearing shall be opened by the filing of the oath of the arbitrator, where required; by the recording of the date, time, and place of the hearing, and the presence of the arbitrator, the parties, and their representatives, if any; and by the receipt by the arbitrator of the statement of the claim and the answering statement, if any.

The arbitrator may, at the beginning of the hearing, ask for statements clarifying the issues involved. In some cases, part or all of the above will have been accomplished at the preliminary hearing conducted by the arbitrator pursuant to Section 10.

The complaining party shall then present evidence to support its claim. The defending party shall then present evidence supporting its defense. Witnesses for each party shall submit to questions or other examination. The arbitrator has the discretion to vary this procedure but shall afford a full and equal opportunity to all parties for the presentation of any material and relevant evidence.

Exhibits, when offered by either party, may be received in evidence by the arbitrator.

The names and addresses of all witnesses and a description of the exhibits in the order received shall be made a part of the record.

There shall be no direct communication between the parties and a neutral arbitrator other than at oral hearings, unless the parties and the arbitrator agree otherwise. Any other oral or written communication from the parties to a neutral arbitrator shall be directed to the AAA for transmittal to the arbitrator.

30. Arbitration in the absence of a party or representative

Unless the law provides to the contrary, the arbitration may proceed in the absence of any party or representative who, after due notice, fails to be present or fails to obtain a postponement. An award shall not be made solely on the default of a party. The arbitrator shall require the party who is present to submit such evidence as the arbitrator may require for the making of an award.

31. Evidence

The parties may offer such evidence as is relevant and material to the dispute and shall produce such evidence as the arbitrator may deem necessary to an understanding and determination of the dispute. An arbitrator or other person authorized by law to subpoena witnesses or documents may do so upon the request of any party or independently.

The arbitrator shall be the judge of the relevance and materiality of the evidence offered, and conformity to legal rules of evidence shall not be necessary. All evidence shall be taken in the presence of all of the arbitrators and all of the parties, except where any of the parties is absent in default or has waived the right.

32. Evidence by affidavits and post-hearing filing of documents or other evidence

The arbitrator may receive and consider the evidence of witnesses by affidavit, but shall give it only such weight as the arbitrator deems it entitled to after consideration of any objection made to its admission.

If the parties agree or the arbitrator directs that documents or other evidence be submitted to the arbitrator after the hearing, the documents or other evidence shall be filed with the AAA for transmission to the arbitrator. All parties shall be afforded an opportunity to examine such documents or other evidence.

33. Inspection or investigation

An arbitrator finding it necessary to make an inspection or investigation in connection with the arbitration shall direct the AAA to so advise the parties. The arbitrator shall set the date and time and the AAA shall notify the parties. Any party who so desires may be present at such an inspection or investigation. In the event that one or all parties are not present at the inspection or investigation, the arbitrator shall make a verbal or written report to the parties and afford them an opportunity to comment.

34. Interim measures

The arbitrator may issue such orders for interim relief as may be deemed necessary to safeguard the property that is the subject matter of the arbitration without prejudice to the rights of the parties or to the final determination of the dispute.

35. Closing of hearing

The arbitrator shall specifically inquire of all parties whether they have any further proofs to offer or witnesses to be heard. Upon receiving negative replies or if satisfied that the record is complete, the arbitrator shall declare the hearing closed and a minute thereof shall be recorded. If briefs are to be filed, the hearing shall be declared closed as of the final date set by the arbitrator for the receipt of briefs. If documents are to be filed as provided in Section 32 and the date set for their receipt is later than that set for the receipt of briefs, the later date shall be the date of closing the hearing. The time limit within which the arbitrator is required to make the award shall commence to run, in the absence of other agreements by the parties, upon the closing of the hearing.

36. Reopening of hearing

The hearing may be reopened on the arbitrator's initiative, or upon application of a party, at any time before the award is made. If reopening the hearing would prevent the making of the award within the specific time agreed on by the parties in the contract(s) out of which the controversy has arisen, the matter may not be reopened unless the parties agree on an extension of time. When no specific date is fixed in the contract, the arbitrator may reopen the hearing and shall have thirty days from the closing of the reopened hearing within which to make an award.

37. Waiver of oral hearing

The parties may provide, by written agreement, for the waiver of oral hearings in any case. If the parties are unable to agree as to the procedure, the AAA shall specify a fair and equitable procedure.

38. Waiver of rules

Any party who proceeds with the arbitration after knowledge that any provision or requirement of these rules has not been complied with and who fails to state an objection thereto in writing shall be deemed to have waived the right to object.

39. Extensions of time

The parties may modify any period of time by mutual agreement. The AAA or the arbitrator may for good cause extend any period of time established by these rules, except the time for making the award.

The AAA shall notify the parties of any extension.

40. Serving of notice

Each party shall be deemed to have consented that any papers, notices, or process necessary or proper for the initiation or continuation of an arbitration under these rules; for any court action in connection therewith; or for the entry of judgment on an award made under these rules may be served on a party by mail addressed to the party or its representative at the last known address or by personal service, in or outside the state where the arbitration is to be held, provided that reasonable opportunity to be heard with regard thereto has been granted to the party.

The AAA and the parties may also use facsimile transmission, telex, telegram, or other written forms of electronic communication to give the notices required by these rules.

41. Time of award

The award shall be made promptly by the arbitrator and, unless otherwise agreed by the parties or specified by law, no later than thirty days from the date of closing the hearing, or, if oral hearings have been waived, from the date of the AAA's transmittal of the final statements and proofs to the arbitrator.

42. Form of award

The award shall be in writing and shall be signed by a majority of the arbitrators. It shall be executed in the manner required by law.

43. Scope of award

The arbitrator may grant any remedy or relief that the arbitrator deems just and equitable and within the scope of the agreement of the parties, including, but not limited to, specific performance of a contract. The arbitrator shall, in the award, assess arbitration fees, expenses, and compensation as provided in Sections 48, 49, and 50 in favor of any party and, in the event that any administrative fees or expenses are due the AAA, in favor of the AAA.

44. Award upon settlement

If the parties settle their dispute during the course of the arbitration, the arbitrator may set forth the terms of the agreed settlement in an award. Such an award is referred to as a consent award.

45. Delivery of award to parties

Parties shall accept as legal delivery of the award the placing of the award or a true copy thereof in the mail addressed to a party or its representative at the last known address, personal service of the award, or the filing of the award in any other manner that is permitted by law.

46. Release of documents for judicial proceedings

The AAA shall, upon the written request of a party, furnish to the party, at its expense, certified copies of any papers in the AAA's possession that may be required in judicial proceedings relating to the arbitration.

47. Applications to court and exclusion of liability

(a) No judicial proceeding by a party relating to the subject matter of the arbitration shall be deemed a waiver of the party's right to arbitrate.

(b) Neither the AAA nor any arbitrator in a proceeding under these rules is a necessary party in judicial proceedings relating to the arbitration.

(c) Parties to these rules shall be deemed to have consented that judgment upon the arbitration award may be entered in any federal or state court having jurisdiction thereof.

(d) Neither the AAA nor any arbitrator shall be liable to any party for any act or omission in connection with any arbitration conducted under these rules.

48. Administrative fee

As a not-for-profit organization, the AAA shall prescribe an Administrative Fee Schedule and a Refund Schedule to compensate it for the cost of providing administrative services. The schedule in effect at the time the demand for arbitration or submission agreement is received shall be applicable.

The administrative fee shall be advanced by the initiating party or parties, subject to final apportionment by the arbitrator in the award.

When a claim or counterclaim is withdrawn or settled, the refund shall be made in accordance with the Refund Schedule.

The AAA may, in the event of extreme hardship on the part of any party, defer or reduce the administrative fee.

49. Expenses

The expenses of witnesses for either side shall be paid by the party producing such witnesses. All other expenses of the arbitration, including required travel and other expenses of the arbitrator, AAA representatives, and any witness and the cost of any proof produced at the direct request of the arbitrator, shall be borne equally by the parties, unless they agree otherwise or unless the arbitrator in the award assesses such expenses or any part thereof against any specified party or parties.

50. Neutral arbitrator's fee

Unless the parties agree otherwise, members of the National Panel of Construction Industry Arbitrators appointed as neutrals will serve without compensation for the first day of service.

Thereafter, compensation shall be based on the amount of service involved and the number of hearings. An appropriate daily rate and other arrangements will be discussed by the administrator with the parties and the arbitrator. If the parties fail to agree to the terms of compensation, an appropriate rate shall be established by the AAA and communicated in writing to the parties.

Any arrangement for the compensation of a neutral arbitrator shall be made through the AAA and not directly between the parties and the arbitrator. The terms of compensation of neutral arbitrators on a panel shall be identical.

51. Deposits

The AAA may require the parties to deposit in advance of any hearings such sums of money as it deems necessary to defray the expense of the arbitration, including the arbitrator's fee, if any, and shall render an accounting to the parties and return any unexpended balance at the conclusion of the case.

52. Interpretation and application of rules

The arbitrator shall interpret and apply these rules insofar as they relate to the arbitrator's powers and duties. When there is more than one arbitrator and a difference arises among them concerning the meaning or application of these rules, it shall be decided by a majority vote. If that is unobtainable, either an arbitrator or a party may refer the question to the AAA for final decision. All other rules shall be interpreted and applied by the AAA.

Expedited procedures

53. Notice by telephone

The parties shall accept all notices from the AAA by telephone. Such notices by the AAA shall subsequently be confirmed in writing to the parties. Should there be a failure to confirm in writing any notice hereunder, the proceeding shall nonetheless be valid if notice has, in fact, been given by telephone.

54. Appointment & qualifications of arbitrator

Where no disclosed claim or counterclaim exceeds $50,000, exclusive of interest and arbitration costs, the AAA shall submit simultaneously to each party an identical list of five proposed arbitrators drawn from the National Panel of Construction Industry Arbitrators, from which one arbitrator shall be appointed.

Each party may strike two names from the list on a peremptory basis. The list is returnable to the AAA within seven days from the date of the AAA's mailing to the parties.

If for any reason the appointment of an arbitrator cannot be made from the list, the AAA may make the appointment from among other members of the panel without the submission of additional lists.

The parties will be given notice by telephone by the AAA of the appointment of the arbitrator, who shall be subject to disqualification for the reasons specified in Section 19. The parties shall notify the AAA, by telephone, within seven days of any objection to the arbitrator appointed. Any objection by a party to the arbitrator shall be confirmed in writing to the AAA with a copy to the other party or parties.

55. Date, time, & place of hearing

The arbitrator shall set the date, time, and place of the hearing. The AAA will notify the parties by telephone, at least seven days in advance of the hearing date. A formal Notice of Hearing will be sent by the AAA to the parties.

56. The hearing

Generally, the hearing shall be completed within one day, unless the dispute is resolved by submission of documents under Section 37. The arbitrator, for good cause shown, may schedule an additional hearing to be held within seven days.

57. Time of award

Unless otherwise agreed by the parties, the award shall be rendered not later than fourteen days from the date of the closing of the hearing.

Administrative fee schedule

A filing fee of $300 will be paid when a case is filed. The balance of the administrative fee is based on the amount of each claim or counterclaim as disclosed when the claim or counterclaim is filed. This balance is due and payable sixty days after the AAA's commencement of administration, or prior to the date of the first hearing, whichever occurs first. If at any time a claim or counterclaim is settled or withdrawn, the balance of the administrative fee remains due and the Refund Schedule shall then be applied. When oral hearings are waived under Section 37, the Administrative Fee Schedule shall still apply.

Amount of claim/counterclaim	Fee
Up to $10,000	$300
10,000 to $25,000	3%
$25,000 to $50,000	$750, plus 2% of excess over $25,000
$50,000 to $100,000	$1,250, plus 1% of excess over $50,000
$100,000 to $500,000	$1,750, plus ½% of excess over $100,000
$500,000 to $5,000,000	$3,750, plus ¼% of excess over $500,000
$5,000,000 to $50,000,000	$15,000, plus ¹⁄₁₀% of excess over $5,000,000

Where the claim or counterclaim exceeds $50 million, there is no additional administrative fee.

When no amount can be stated at the time of filing, the administrative fee is $1,000, subject to adjustment in accordance with the above schedule as soon as an amount can be disclosed.

An appropriate administrative fee will be determined by the AAA for claims and counterclaims that are not for a monetary amount.

If there are more than two parties represented in the arbitration, an additional 10% of the administrative fee will be due for each additional represented party.

The minimum administrative fee for a case heard by three arbitrators is $1,500, payable by the party requesting same.

Postponement fees

Sole-arbitrator cases

$100 is payable by a party causing its first postponement of any scheduled hearing.

$200 is payable by a party causing its second or subsequent postponement of any scheduled hearing.

Three-arbitrator cases

$150 is payable by a party causing its first postponement of any scheduled hearing.

$300 is payable by a party causing its second or subsequent postponement of any scheduled hearing.

Additional hearing fee

$75 is payable by each party for each hearing after the first hearing that is clerked by the AAA.

Hearing-room rental

Hearing rooms for second and subsequent hearings are available on a rental basis at AAA offices. Check with your local office for specific availability and rates.

Refund schedule

The Refund Schedule is based on the administrative fee due on a claim or counterclaim asserted by a party.

If the AAA is notified that a claim or counterclaim has been settled or withdrawn before a list of arbitrators has been sent out, all of the fee in excess of $300 will be refunded. If the AAA is notified that a claim or counterclaim has been settled or withdrawn after a list of arbitrators has been sent out but before the original due date for the return of the first list, two thirds of the fee in excess of $300 will be refunded.

If the AAA is notified that a claim or counterclaim has been settled or withdrawn after the original due date for the return of the first list but at least two business days before the initial date and time set for the first scheduled hearing, one third of the fee in excess of $300 will be refunded.

There will be no refund after any hearing or mediation conference has been held; where a claim or counterclaim was filed as an undetermined/undisclosed claim and remained so at the time of settlement or withdrawal; where a consent award was issued by the arbitrator; or where a determination is made by the arbitrator resulting in the closing of the file.

Glossary

aesthetic zoning Zoning requirements based totally on architectural or visual aspects of a building.

American Arbitration Association A not-for-profit organization that exists for the purpose of facilitating arbitration. This entity is often referred to as the triple A or AAA.

American Institute of Architects Commonly referred to as the A.I.A. This association for architects produces standard contracts, agreements, specifications, and many forms that are commonly used in the construction industry.

arbitration A method of dispute resolution whereby the parties choose a neutral person (an arbitrator) to settle a disagreement rather than use the court system. This method of arbitration can be provided for in the contract or can be chosen after a dispute has arisen.

area variance A permitted change in zoning with respect to dimensional matters such as the distance a house must be from the property line, the overall height of the structure, etc. This change in zoning is allowed under the condition when a house is in violation of inches or a foot or two of the allowable distance to the side or front of the property and to enforce the zoning ordinance to the letter of the law would be unjust.

articles of incorporation A document that must be filled out and filed with the state to request corporate status. Information to be included in this document includes purpose of the business, number of shares issued, value of the shares, address of the corporation etc.

assault The threatening of a person for the purpose of putting that person in fear of imminent danger.

American Society of Testing Materials Known as ASTM. This organization provides test methods and minimum standards for a wide array of products and materials.

attorney-client privilege A court rule that allows a client the right to prevent an attorney from divulging information provided by the client in confidence.

battery The causing of a harmful or offensive contact with the body of a person.

breach of contract Failure by a party to a contract to carry out the terms and conditions of the contract.

bylaws The rules that the corporation has voluntarily adopted to be governed by. Bylaws include how, when and where shareholders can vote, how the board of directors is elected, etc.

case of first impression Litigation where the subject matter of the trial has never been decided by a judge in any previous case; a situation where no prior cases have ruled on the issue in controversy.

causation The reason that a detrimental event has occurred.

caveat emptor A legal doctrine that puts the buyer in a position that the object of a sale is being purchased in an "as-is" condition and any defects are the buyer's problem. Also known as *buyer beware*.

chancery court A specific division of the court system that exists for the purpose of hearing special types of cases, including mechanic's lien actions.

chattel Personal property; property that is not real estate. Construction equipment, tools and material are personal property of the construction company.

claims The accusation that a person or entity harmed or otherwise caused damage to another party.

closely held corporation A corporation where the shares are held by a very small group of individuals, usually from one family.

common law Law that is created by judges in circumstances where the government has failed to pass a law on the subject matter in question.

compensatory damages Damages paid to an injured party only to make repayment for the injuries caused. *See punitive damages and nominal damages.*

conditional zoning A change in zoning that requires that some action be taken before the change will be permitted. Such changes are suspect because they may lead to "back-room" deals with zoning officials.

consideration Something of value given by a party as their contribution to the contract. For example, in the sale of property, the consideration by one party is the money to be paid to the seller, whereas the passing of the title of the property by the seller to the buyer is the consideration by the other party. Usually both parties must provide consideration for there to be a valid contract.

construction industry arbitration rules Arbitration rules set by the American Arbitration Association (AAA)—an organization established to promote the use of arbitration to settle disputes. These rules specifically address the construction industry problems.

conversion Illegally, and without permission, taking control of someone's property. Stealing a car would be conversion of the property of the car owner.

corporation An artificial entity created by the state governments to allow a business to have an identity that is separate from the owners. This split identity protects the personal assets of the owners of the corporation from creditors of the corporation.

counterclaims A counter-suit against the plaintiff. In the typical lawsuit, the plaintiff makes a claim against the defendant for damages; if the defendant makes a claim against the plaintiff, it is called a counterclaim.

counteroffer A modified version of an offer. An offer is a proposal by one party to another party for the purposes of entering into a contract. If the party receiving the offer refuses it and submits an altered version of the offer, it is called a counteroffer.

cross-examination The process of questioning a witness during trial by an attorney on the opposing side of the case.

deed A legal document that transfers ownership of land.

default The failure of a party to comply with the terms of a contract.

defendant The party being sued and accused of committing some wrong action by the plaintiff.

deposition Questioning of a witness or party to a lawsuit. The questioning is performed with the person under oath, and the deposition is one method of discovery.

detour Used in the legal arena to denote a non-work-related minor change in a work-related job or errand. A delivery person who stops at home between deliveries is considered to be on a detour. Employers may be liable for negligent acts of the employee during a detour.

detrimental reliance In regards to a contract, one party is trusting that the other party will comply with the terms of the contract when the other party has no intentions to comply with these terms. An injustice is the result.

direct examination The questioning of a witness by the attorney whom requested that the witness come to testify. *See cross examination*.

discovery A method of obtaining information from the opposing party to a lawsuit. The rules for discovery are provided by both the legislature and judges. Discovery methods include depositions, interrogatories, and production of documents. Failure to comply with discovery may result in sanctions against the offending attorney.

damages The payment of compensation to a person physically or financially injured.

duty A legal obligation to act or refrain from acting in a certain manner.

duty of care *See duty.*

dying declaration An exception to the hearsay rule. The statement of a person who believes that death is imminent can be repeated at trial by a witness to the statement. The person who made the dying declaration must have died or is unable to testify.

easement A right given by the owner of land to another person to use the property.

easement by necessity An easement provided by law that gives the right of egress over the property of another. This easement is allowed when a piece of property is surrounded by property and has no access to any roads.

easement by prescription Acquiring the right to use someone's land by using the land uninterrupted for a very long time. For example, if a person crossed over the land of another for many years, a judge may grant them the continued right to cross this property despite the landowner's objections.

essential terms The information that must be contained in a contract for it to be considered valid. Essential terms may include price, quality, date of delivery, etc.

excited utterance An exception to the hearsay rule. If a person exclaimed something while under the stress of an exciting event, it could be repeated in court by a witness to the statement. Excited utterances are allowed to be considered as evidence. *See hearsay.*

exculpatory Describes language in a contract whereby a party will not be held liable for their own negligent acts.

expedited arbitration Allows for a quicker resolution process when the amount in controversy is considered small.

expert witness A person who has significant experience or education in a particular subject and is allowed to testify for the purposes of assisting the judge or jury in understanding a complex issue.

express contract An agreement where the terms are explicitly stated by language.

express grant An easement provided by a valid written document.

false imprisonment Detaining or restraining a person without a legal right to do so.

fiduciary A person who, based on his/her position, has a special duty to act in a certain manner with respect to the client or partner. An attorney must always act in the best interest of the client and is therefore a fiduciary of the client. A partner is a fiduciary of the partnership and must always act in the best interest of the partnership.

foreign corporation A corporation that is not registered in the state where a controversy has arisen. A business incorporated in one state is considered a foreign corporation in any of the other forty-nine states.

foreseeability The predictability that an action will produce a particular detrimental result.

fraud A false representation of the facts by one party of the contract to the other party. The presence of fraud in a contract is usually grounds for voiding the contract and making it unenforceable.

frolic Used in the legal sense to denote a non-work-related major change in a work-related errand. A delivery person who leaves a predetermined travel route to spend a week in Florida is on a frolic. Employers are usually not liable for negligent acts that occur while the employee is on a frolic.

general contractor Denotes (in the construction industry) a construction company that has contracted directly with the owner and is responsible for a satisfactory completion of the construction project.

hearsay The repeating of a statement by a testifying witness that was not uttered by the testifying witness. Statements where the witness repeats something someone else said are not allowed as evidence.

husband-wife privilege A privelege extended to married couples that says that neither spouse can be forced to testify against the other.

impeach The discrediting of a witness by showing inconsistencies in the previous statements of the witness.

implied contracts An agreement recognized by the courts as being binding on the parties even though there was no formal agreement. The consenting to the terms of the agreement is implied by the parties' actions.

implied warranty A guarantee that the item sold meets some level of quality established by industry standards. This guarantee is not provided in the written terms of the contract but is implied by law.

indemnification A contractual agreement where one party agrees to be responsible for any problem caused by the other party.

intentional tort A cognizant failure to act as one should; an action that is wrong as a matter of law that a person violates by choice.

interrogatories Questions asked by a party to a lawsuit to the opposing party. These questions must be answered under oath. Interrogatories are one method of discovery. *See discovery.*

lack of capacity Legal terminology that denotes when a person is unqualified mentally to be entering into contracts. Those with lack of capacity include minors, the mentally disturbed, and those under the influence of drugs.

land A piece of real estate; a plot of property.

license When a landowner grants temporary privilege to someone to enter on the land of the owner. An electrician has a license to enter on the property to perform electrical repairs requested by the owner.

lien A claim against property to satisfy an unpaid debt.

limited partner A partner in a business whose liability is limited to the amount the limited partner has invested. In essence, this limits the amount a limited partner can lose.

liquidated damages Fees assessed against the contractor for failure to complete a construction project before the scheduled completion date.

litigation A lawsuit for the purpose of settling a dispute.

mechanic's lien A law created by the legislature that provides a priority interest in a piece of property for the purposes of obtaining payment for construction services.

merchant A person involved in the sale of goods; refers to someone who sells products at the wholesale or retail level.

mirror image rule A rule in contract law that requires that a person accept a contract exactly as it was offered. If a person alters the terms of an offer and attempts to accept the offer, it is not a valid acceptance under the mirror image rule.

mistake in fact In the context of an arbitration hearing, the situation where the arbitrator improperly determines what the facts of the case are.

mistake in judgement In the context of an arbitration hearing, the situation where the arbitrator misapplies the applicable law.

moral turpitude Describes a person whose actions are considered unethical and against public policy.

motions When a party to a lawsuit officially requests that the judge take some action. A motion for a dismissal would be a request to have a lawsuit dismissed. A motion for a time extension would be a request to the judge for more time to do something.

negligence Failure to act as a reasonable person would act under similar circumstances.

no-lien clause Language in a construction contract that forbids the filing of any mechanic's liens by any of the contractors, subcontractors, or suppliers. These clauses may be unenforceable in some states.

nominal consideration A situation where there is a gross disparity in the value of the exchange in a contract. The payment of ten dollars for a new car is obviously too small and would be treated as a nominal consideration.

nominal damages A damage award that is extremely small because the actual damage to the injured party was not substantial. The fact that damages were awarded, although nominal, show that the plaintiff was in the right.

nonconforming use Exceptions to the zoning plan for land uses that were preexisting prior to the latest zoning plan. These exceptions are allowed because the enforcing of the new zoning would be an extreme hardship on the present owner.

non goods Denotes services as opposed to products.

nonmerchant A purchaser or seller of a product who is not normally active in the wholesale or retail of the product. Often used to refer to a consumer.

Occupational Safety and Health Administration A branch of the United States government, Department of Labor, OSHA, that is responsible for enforcing rules to protect the safety of employees. This agency provides a detailed set of safety rules for the construction industry. Failure to comply with OSHA would possibly result in sanctions.

partnership An agreement between two or more people to partake in a business enterprise for the purpose of making a profit.

past consideration When the giving up of something of value took place before the contract became effective. Thus, the item is considered past consideration.

piercing the corporate veil The losing of the corporate status. A business obtains corporate status for the purpose of protecting the personal assets of the business owners. Corporate status can only be maintained if the appropriate rules are followed. If the rules are not followed, then corporate status is taken away.

plaintiff The party that initiates a lawsuit. It typically is the injured party.

pretrial The time frame that begins when a lawsuit is filed and ends on the day trial begins. This time is used for the parties to the lawsuit to posture their defenses and offenses.

punitive damages Damages awarded to an injured party for the sole purpose of punishing the defendant.

quit claim deed A deed that guarantees nothing about past or present ownership. *See deed*.

reasonable person A standard that is set by judges, by which they compare the way defendant behaved to that of an average person.

request to admit A request by one party that the other party admit the existence of a fact prior to the start of trial. Such admissions reduce the amount of items that must be proved at trial.

request to produce A request by one party that the other party provide documents or other evidence. Requests to produce are one method of discovery.

retainage A percentage of the amount due under the contract, usually 5 or 10 percent, that is held by the owner pending satisfactory completion of the project. Owners may hold on to the retainage for several months after the project is complete to cover the costs of repairs of any faulty construction.

S corporation A corporate status that provides small companies with the benefits of being a corporation without subjecting the company to corporate taxes. Owners of an S corporation are taxed as sole proprietorships.

shareholders A person who owns a portion of a company. Also called a stockholder.

silent partner An investor in a business who provides working capital or property but does not participate in the administration of the company's day to day affairs.

sole proprietorship A business where one individual personally owns all the assets of the business. A sole proprietor takes personal responsibility for all the liabilities of the business.

special use An option provided by the zoning board that provides for a different zoning than the property presently has. Special uses are permitted exceptions for zoning changes that have a benefit to society as a whole (i.e., hospitals, churches etc.).

specific performance The requirement that a certain act be done rather than assessing damages. For example, in a real estate transaction a party may request that a breaching seller transfer title. That is, the injured party is requiring that the seller specifically perform their part of the contract. Specific performance is very common in the breach of real estate contracts.

spot zoning The change in zoning for one single piece of property that is surrounded by other pieces of property with zoning inconsistent with the change allowed to the single parcel. Such zoning is usually not acceptable.

statute of frauds A law whereby certain contracts are not valid unless the contract is in writing.

strict tort liability A theory of culpability in which one who manufactures a defective product is responsible for any injuries caused by that product.

subcontractor A construction company hired by the general contractor to perform only a portion of the construction project. A subcontractor usually has one specific trade (plumber, carpentry, electrical).

summary judgement A motion presented to the court stating that the parties are not in disagreement with regards to the facts and therefore the case should be resolved by the judge determining who is right as a matter of law.

tort An action by which one party caused physical or financial damage to another party in a situation that does not involve a contract.

tortfeaser One who commits any of the various types of torts.

trespass Illegal use, interference, or entry on the land of another.

unconscionable contract An agreement that is so unfair to one party that a judge refuses to enforce it.

Uniform Commercial Code Commonly referred to as the U.C.C. This code is a uniform set of rules to guide commercial transactions involving goods.

unilateral mistake A misunderstanding by only one of the party to a contract. A bilateral mistake would be a misunderstanding by both of the parties.

use variance An allowable change in zoning to allow the property to be used for something different than the original zoning.

valid offer An offer is a proposal by one party to another party to enter into a contract.

variances An allowable change in zoning for a requirement that if enforced would be grossly unfair or impractical.

vicarious liability When the results of the action of one person are the responsibility of another. An employer may be vicariously liable for the negligence of the employee.

voire dire The questioning of a potential jury member for the purpose of determining if it would be appropriate to add the person to the jury.

warranty deed A deed that guarantees that the seller is the exclusive owner of the property ownership. *See deed*.

Index

About the author

Dr. August W. Domel, Jr., is a licensed Structural Engineer, Professional Engineer, and Attorney at Law in Illinois specializing in failure investigation and construction law. Currently he is an Adjunct Assistant Professor at the Illinois Institute of Technology (I.I.T.), teaching construction management and construction law courses.

He graduated Summa Cum Laude from Bradley University with a bachelor of science degree in civil engineering. He received a masters degree and Ph.D. in civil engineering from I.I.T. and the University of Illinois at Chicago, respectively. He also earned a law degree from Loyola University of Chicago.

He has written books on the topics of earthquake design of high-rise buildings, design of water retaining structures, concrete floor design, and estimating. Most recently he co-authored *Residential Contracting: Hands-on Project Management for the Builders*, published by McGraw-Hill.